Mark Leigh continues to think of himself as a teenager despite having reached the age when inserting his birth year on online forms, he has to scroll much further down the list than he'd like. Pouring himself into skinny jeans, wearing an on-trend Liberty X T-shirt and the mandatory back-to-front baseball cap, Mark conducted his extensive research for *How to Talk Teen* by going undercover.

Infiltrating teen gangs and hanging out with teenage girls, however, was not without its problems but fortunately, by the time the restraining order was issued, he'd collected sufficient examples of slang and its usage to fill this book.

Mark has written or co-written fifty-five humour and trivia books on subjects as diverse as celebrities, extra-terrestrials, swearing pets, the Conservative party and toilets (the last two topics were unrelated). He lives in Surrey with his family and dog and, when he's not writing or chillin' with teenagers, steals pens and A4 photocopier paper from his job in marketing.

For more details visit www.mark-leigh.com

How To Talk Teen

Mark Leigh

ROBINSON

ROBINSON

First published in Great Britain in 2016 by Robinson

Text copyright © Mark Leigh, 2016
Illustrations copyright © Dominic Trevett

1 3 5 7 9 8 6 4 2

A CIP catalogue record for this book
is available from the British Library.

ISBN 978-1-47213-744-9 (paperback)

Typeset in Frutiger by TW Type, Cornwall
Printed and bound in Great Britain by Clays Ltd, St Ives plc
Papers used by Robinson are from well-managed forests and other responsible
sources

MIX
Paper from
responsible sources
FSC
www.fsc.org   FSC® C104740

Robinson
is an imprint of
Little, Brown Book Group
Carmelite House
50 Victoria Embankment
London EC4Y 0DZ

An Hachette UK Company
www.hachette.co.uk

www.littlebrown.co.uk

Introduction

This book is out of date.

My bad.

The thing with slang is that it's always evolving, and the slang that changes the most is teenage slang. What's on trend one day is suddenly sooo last month. Some words or phrases, for example, have the lifespan of a mayfly (or a boy band).

That means you're riding the struggle bus just trying to keep up.

So, here's the thing. *How to Talk Teen* is primarily designed to entertain. If you were expecting a treatise into sociological and linguistic trends you'll be disappointed and probably MAF.

What it is, however, is a collection of current (as current as production deadlines allow) popular slang as used by teenagers.

'Is it a definitive list?' you ask. Yeah, right. Trying to do this is almost unpossible for a whole ton of reasons. For starters, the slang used by someone in year eight will be remarkably different from the slang used by someone graduating from uni.

Then there's the regional differences which can be gimongous. What might be popular slang in Manchester might be unheard of in Birmingham. Or it might be passé in Newcastle or have a totes different meaning in Liverpool. Even different parts of London use completely different slang.

And if that's not divisive enough, then consider the different teen social groups or subcultures. Thirteen-year-old girls for instance, won't have a great dealio in common with wannabe gangstas.

And on to the words themselves . . . Some of the terms in

the book have entered common usage. Some were teen slang to begin with but have been appropriated by grown-ups. Some words have fallen out of favour but have recently seen a revival. Some are used exclusively for texting/emailing as opposed to being spoken. And vice versa.

A lot of the slang is US in origin but has made its way to the UK, sometimes several years after first being adopted over there. Some slang involves the word being used ironically while other words or phrases have different meanings (sometimes the two sentiments are the complete opposite; go figure!).

So, chillax, take off your kicks and decompress. After immersing yourself in its contents you too will be capable and confident enough to differentiate between YOLO and YOYO or a mofo and a FoCo and truly understand how to talk teen.

Mark Leigh
Surrey, England, 2016

PS Some of the slang in this book might be considered politically incorrect and/or involves expletives but hey, that's teenagers for you.

Thanks

A big shout out to my mains who suggested words and phrases for inclusion without any expectation whatsoever that they would receive a free copy of this book in return:

Andrew Brown, James Brown, Michele Davis, Kane Hearne, John Holland, Sara Howell, Kitty Jones, Alec Laurent, Barney Leigh, Polly Leigh, Mary Myzer, Simon Safran, Emily Sandford, Emma Simon and Allie Taylor.

A

Abercrazy (adjective, noun)

Anyone who's infatuated with [...] and who goes out of their way to [...] and buy clothes in a shop that [...]
See also, Abercrombie.

Abercrombie (noun)

Somebody devoid of personality [...] who only buys clothes from [...] in anticipation that they look [...] so much viewed as people [...]
See also, Abercrazy.

Absofuckinglutely (adverb)

Something that is so exceptional it is [...] absolutely absolute.

Addy (noun)

Short for address, usually email [...]

Adorbs/adorbz (adjective)

Cute, petite, attractive, delightful [...] Usually preceded by the word [...]

Abercrazy (adjective, noun)

Anyone who's infatuated with clothes from Abercrombie & Fitch and who goes out of their way to defend the experience of trying to buy clothes in a shop that is marginally less gloomy than a cave.
   See also, *Aberzombie*

Aberzombie (noun)

Somebody devoid of personality and any individual style, who only buys clothes from Abercrombie & Fitch under the misapprehension that they look *über* cool. Aberzombies are not so much viewed as people, but brain-dead, walking mannequins.
   See also, *Abercrazy*

Absofuckinglutely (adverb, interjection)

Something that is so exceptionally certain or definite that it is absolutely absolute.

Addy (noun)

Short for address; usually email rather than postal.

Adorbs/adorbz (adjective)

Cute, petite, attractive, delightful or charming. In effect, adorable. Usually preceded by the word *totes*.

Aberzombie

Adorkable (adjective)

A term of endearment for somebody who is considered adorable because of their gawky, clumsy, awkward or otherwise *dorky* characteristics.

AF (adverb)

Completely/totally: an abbreviation welcomed universally by anyone too lazy to type or say the words 'as fuck'. By the time this book is published it will have probably been shortened still to just 'A'.

E.g. 'Man. I got to bed at three this morning. It's 4 p.m. and I'm still as tired AF.'

AFK (interjection)

Away from keyboard. What to type when the online conversation you're involved in is so riveting that you have to take a short break to stop yourself getting over-excited. Sometimes followed by BRB.

See also, *BRB, BRBx*

Ah-mazing/Ahh-mazing/Ahhh-mazing, etc. (adjective)

Something or someone that is more amazing that amazing… but doesn't quite qualify as being *awesome.*

A-hole (noun)

A polite way of calling someone an asshole; someone whose character traits include (but are not restricted to) being obnoxious, mean, dumb, rude, hateful, aggressive, selfish, arrogant, loud-mouthed and belligerent.

See also, *Asshole, Asshole Points, Assholic, Douche, Douchebag, Tool, Tool bag, Wanker*

Aight (adverb, adjective)

A way to say 'all right' (i.e. a sign of agreement, satisfaction or comprehension) in a *hip* and *ghetto* way. Rhymes with 'tight'.

Air five (noun, verb)

A *high five* greeting made where the other person is too far away to make physical contact, e.g. from across a room or while having a phone conversation.

See also *Wi-five*

Airplane mode (noun)

The act of cutting yourself off from all forms of electronic communication and, in effect, disconnecting yourself from your social circle. There are usually two reasons for entering airplane mode: (1) a new boyfriend or (2) a new girlfriend.

E.g. 'Dan dumped her and she's been in airplane mode for a week.'

ALAB (verb)

Someone who is 'acting like a bitch'.

Alcoholiday (noun)

(a) Taking a day off school or work as a result of a massive hangover.
(b) Taking a day off school or work because you intend to spend that day drinking.
(c) A length of time spent at a bar or a party etc., heavily drinking, e.g. 'Here's to a six-hour alcoholiday!'
(d) Any event or public holiday that provides a good excuse for drinking, e.g. Christmas, New Year's Eve, St Patrick's Day, Lent.

Allow (interjection)

The opposite of what you might think this means, responding to a question or statement with 'allow' actually infers that you definitely *do not* want to do what's just been suggested. In other words, 'Hell no!' or 'Fuck that shit.'

E.g.

Friend: 'Let's enrol in summer school so we'll be better prepared for GCSEs.'

You: 'Allow that!'

Alpha geek (noun)

The most computer literate/tech savvy person in a work environment.

E.g. 'Eric's the alpha geek here. What he doesn't know about electromagnetic radiation and wave particle duality isn't worth shit'.

See also, *Dork, Dorky, Geek*

All that (adjective)

While this term can refer to something that is superior in looks or ability, it is more commonly used to describe someone who acts or thinks they're superior – without any justification whatsoever.

E.g.

Girl one: 'Look at her with her with her skinny jeans and her Mac makeup and her red heels. She think she all that, but she not.'

Girl two: 'Skank.'

See also, *All that and a bag of chips*

All that and a bag of chips (adjective)

Something that is superior to merely being *all that*.

TATTOO

Alt girl

Alt girl (noun)

Also known as alternative chicks, alt girls sport piercings, *tats*, brightly coloured hair and an unconventional fashion sense and/or music preference. Alt girls are definitely not the girl-next-door . . . unless you happen to live next door to a tattoo parlour or goth club.

· **Amazeballs** (adjective)

Used to describe someone or something that is incredible, awesome or cool – or which causes great surprise or sudden wonder. Ironically, most things labelled amazeballs usually aren't.
  See also, *Cool, Dope, Hip, Kickass, Killer, Savage, Swag*

Amp'd/amp'd up/amped (verb)

To be so excited, *hyper* and ready for action that you're visibly shaking in anticipation.
  See also, *Pumped, Psyched, Stoked*

An' shit/and shit (adverb)

Added to the end of a sentence, this phrase works in two ways:
  (a) A method to end that sentence when you don't actually know what to say. In this way it takes the place of the words 'etcetera, etcetera . . .' E.g. 'For the new term I bought a new set square, a protractor, a compass an' shit.'
  (b) A way of making any statement sound tougher. E.g. 'I had this dream about a fluffy kitten sliding down a glowing rainbow an' shit.'

Anticipointment (noun)

The sick feeling that comes after eagerly looking forward to something that subsequently fails appallingly to meet any of your expectations.
  E.g. '*Terminator Genisys? Terminator* anticipointment!'

Ape/Apeshit (adjective)

A state of intense anger and uncontrollable rage. This condition usually manifests itself in losing all sense of reason and shouting the word fuck a lot.

NB. Not to be confused with being or going *batshit*.

Arsed (verb)

Bothered; usually used in the past tense and proceeded by the words 'can't be' or 'couldn't be' to express a complete lack of interest in making an effort to complete a task or action.

Arsed up (verb)

To get annoyed or wound up about something.

Askhole (noun)

(a) Someone who asks a succession of pointless and/or stupid questions because either they want to prove they understand what's being discussed or because they have absolutely no idea what's being discussed.

(b) Someone who asks for advice and then proceeds to ignore it, or actually do the complete opposite.

E.g.

Friend: 'What time shall we leave for the airport?'

You: 'Well, there's road works and the traffic's gonna be heavy so I reckon we need to leave yours at 8 a.m. latest.'

Friend: 'Sounds good.' [To minicab company on phone] 'Hello. Can we order a cab for 9 tomorrow morning?'

You: 'Askhole.'

Assed out (adjective)

(a) To be extremely tired/exhausted; e.g. 'I was so assed out I overslept and missed my interview at Maccy D's.'

(b) To lose out on something; to be out of luck – e.g. 'You know that job at Maccy D's? I assed out.'

Asshat (adjective or noun)

General purpose derogative term for someone who is stupid, pretentious, pompous, or self-absorbed. Derives from the notion that this type of person goes around with their head inserted far up their bottom.

Asshole (noun)

See *a-hole*

Asshole Points, AP (noun)

Just as *swag points* compare how 'cool' anyone is, asshole points are awarded for being a *douche*.

Assholic (adjective, noun)

Someone who perpetually acts like an asshole. Also a term to describe this type of behaviour.

Assne (noun)

Acne found on the buttocks and lower back.
   See also, *Bacne/Backne, Chestne, Rackne*

Awesome (adjective)

Used when 'fantastic' or 'brilliant' just won't do. However, because anything can be described as 'awesome' (e.g. hair, snogging, guitar solos, shops, ice cream, jobs, gigs, jeans, *Simpsons* episodes, snakes, holidays, beer, cars, skateboard stunts, movies, pizzas and socks), the potency of the word has become somewhat diminished.
   See also, *Cool, Dope, Fly, Hip*

Awesomesauce/awesome sauce (adjective)

If you mixed 'astounding' with 'astonishing' and added a hint of 'amazing' you'd end up with awesomesauce. This is the pure, unadulterated essence of 'devastating' and is used to describe anything that is way, way, way, way, way, way, way, way more awesome than mere *awesome*.

Awkfest (noun)

An embarrassing situation involving more than two people.

E.g. 'So we're the only ones dressed as Spongebob Squarepants at this memorial service. What a total awkfest!'

Awkward turtle (noun)

A situation in which something awkward happens and everyone present is aware of the awkwardness. The phrase is accompanied by the awkward turtle gesture; putting one hand on top of the other to make a shell shape, then rotating one's thumbs so they resemble turtle flippers.

E.g.

Girl one: 'Kris is the absolute worst kisser ever. He ended up almost licking my entire face!'

Kris: 'Hey. I'm right behind you, you know.'

Girl two: 'Awkward turtle.'

[Everyone laughs. Well, apart from Kris.]

Awky/awkie/awkies (adjective)

A particularly uncomfortable or embarrassing situation. Sometimes followed by the words mo (moment) or *sitch*.

E.g.

Girl one: 'So I wrote this really graphic text about what I'd like to do to him but accidentally sent it to my cousin who's also called Wayne!'

Girl two: 'Awkie mo!'

Girl one: 'I know! But then he replied that he felt exactly the same way about me!'

Girl two: 'Totes awky mo!'

Babystalk (verb)

To look through someone's oldest Facebook photos to see what someone looked like when they were young.

E.g. 'I babystalked him the other day. Braces and zits. Not a good look!'

Back in the day (interjection)

Referring to a time when mobile phones had keypads, the best gaming experience was a Sega Dreamcast and everyone had a copy of *Popstars* by *Hear'Say*.

Bacne/Backne (noun)

Acne that covers the back.

See also, *Assne, Chestne, Rackne*

Bad (noun)

Something or someone that is cool and/or incredibly attractive/sexy.

See also, *Dope, Fit, Fly, Hip, Killer, Tight*

Badass (noun)

Someone with supreme confidence who reeks of cool and plays by his own rules. Usually has contempt for authority and a *DGAF* attitude in absolutely everything he does. Badder than a *bad boy* but nowhere near as bad as a *BAMF*.

See also, *Bad Boy, BAMF*

Bad boy or **Badboy** (noun)

Viewed by some girls as an attractive character trait, a bad boy is someone who doesn't give a rat's ass what people think of him but more importantly, doesn't conform to accepted standards of behaviour. While this can cover many aspects of conduct and lifestyle, e.g. appearance, attitude, drink and drug usage, respect for authority, not tying shoelaces, personal hygiene etc., a bad boy can be easily identified if parents answer, 'No fucking way!' to the following question: 'Would you want your daughter to date him?'

See also, *Badass, BAMF*

Badical (adjective)

When you need a word to describe something that's so *bad* (or *badass*) yet *cool* at the same time. Or if you can't decide if something is bad or radical . . . but want to give an opinion.

E.g. 'Did you see that hack he came up with for *Minecraft* survival mode? That was so badical!'

Bae (noun)

Pronounced 'bay', this is a term of endearment, usually referring to a boyfriend or girlfriend and, crucially, 25 per cent shorter than the more traditional term that it's usurped, 'babe'. Essential when you have limited time to refer to your significant other.

Baggable (adjective)

Describing someone who has a great body but whose face is *bugly.* The inference is that the only way you'd have sex with them is if they were wearing a bag over their head.

See also, *Bodybag, Bugly, Butters, Dugly, Fugly*

Bail (verb)

To leave somewhere, either because it's so dull or *basic* or because of a better opportunity elsewhere; to withdraw from a social event at short notice.

See also, *Dip/dip out, Ghost/ghosting*

Bail-out call (noun)

The call your date doesn't believe for a moment but which gives you a reason to leave early. Bail-out calls tend to be made because the date isn't going the way you hoped or because the guy's a real *creep*.

E.g.

Girl one: 'So I called Lisa and pretended to be the police and told her that her family had all been killed in a train crash that specifically won't be mentioned on the news.'

Girl two: 'Good bail-out call'

See also, *Date bail*

BAMF (noun)

Bad-assed motherfucker. Someone who demonstrates extremely reckless or violent behaviour and utter contempt for the consequences. As a comparison; somebody who shoplifts is a *bad boy*. Someone who steals a car is a *badass*. Someone who steals a police car and then crashes it into two more police cars is a BAMF.

See also, *Badass, Bad boy.*

Bang (verb)

(a) To ignore a phone call.
(b) Crowded.
(c) To be stoned or high.
(d) To have sex.
(e) To beat someone up severely.

E.g.

Friend: 'You banged my call, dude!'

You: 'The party was so bang I couldn't hear you. Anyway, I was well banged and was banging Steph when her *BF* caught us and banged me to within an inch of my life.'

Bangin'/banging

Something that is loud, impressive or *awesome*. Can also refer to someone who is incredibly attractive or sexy.

E.g.

You: 'Awesome party!'

Friend: 'Yeah. Bangin' DJ. Bangin' sounds. Bangin' hot tub. Bangin' girls.'

You: 'Bangin'.'

See also, *Lit, Poppin'*

Bang on trend (adjective)

Something that is more up-to-the-minute and fashionable than just merely being *on trend*.

See also, *Cool, Hip, On trend, Trending*

Bank (adjective, verb)

This can mean a serious amount of money or being incredibly wealthy.

E.g. 'My cuz won the lotto. Now he's got serious bank', 'Have you seen her apartment? She must be totally banked.'

See also, *Ends, Mad stacks*

Bantz (noun, verb)

Like biz, cuz and Jay-Z, the 'z' at the end of this word makes this a far cooler way of saying 'banter' and refers to a playful and friendly way of exchanging teasing remarks. Can also be used to describe how two people have a mutual understanding or empathy with each other.

E.g. 'Me, Danny, Mikey and Ghostface. We got the bantz!'

Warning: If you are skilled in teasing or mocking your friends it's important to resist all temptation to call yourself Bantersaurus Rex or the Archbishop of Banterbury. Use these phrases and you'll score maximum *Asshole points.*

See also, *Rip the piss out of/rip the shit out of, Shantz* and *Top bantz.*

Bare (adjective)

An excessive amount of something.

E.g.

You: 'Dude! My cupboards are bare!'

Friend: 'You got no food?'

You: 'No, man. I mean I got loads of cupboards!'

Friend: 'Oh.'

Barf (verb)

To puke up.

See also, *Ralph, Upchuck*

Basic (adjective)

Something or someone that is unsophisticated, stupid, unoriginal, boring or uncool. Can also be used to describe something that takes place that is sooo predictable.

E.g.

You: 'Nadeen was flashing her titties at the party.'

Friend: 'Yeah. So basic.'

See also, *Lame*

Batshit (adjective)

Term used to describe someone who demonstrates completely irrational behaviour and/or a level of insanity that is beyond mere *cray cray* but not as severe as *MAF*. For emphasis batshit is sometimes used as a prefix to the following words: bonkers, crazy, insane.

Beast (adjective, noun)

Someone who absolutely excels at an activity or something that is truly exceptional.
   Example one: 'Did you see that goal by Neymar? He's an absolute beast in the box.'
   Example two: 'That goal was so beast!'
   See also, *Boss, Epic, Prime*

Beat face (adjective, noun)

Someone whose make-up is so perfect they look absolutely *awesome.*

Beautimous (adjective)

More than just being beautiful, this describes someone or something that is both extremely attractive and fabulous (or gorgeous).

Beautimous maximus (adjective)

To be even more stunningly beautiful than being mere *beautimous.*

Beef (noun)

An argument or a grudge; can also mean the fight itself which inevitably occurs after the initial beef.

E.g.

Friend: 'I told you I was vegan. Why you serving me this shit?'

You: 'Hey, quit getting into a beef about beef!'

Beer goggs/beer goggles (noun)

A condition of the eyes caused by excessive consumption of beer, the result of which is that members of the opposite sex appear far more sexually attractive than they actually are.

Begfriend/beg friend (noun)

Someone you don't really know and don't really like, who hangs around you and your *mains*, hoping to be accepted into your *squad*, sometimes just because they want to take advantage of you.

See also, *Frenemy, Suck up*

Belidge/bellidge (adjective)

A state of drunkenness that causes a person to become confrontational and argumentative . . . but not yet violent. Contraction of 'belligerent'.

Bestest (adjective)

The best of the best; the ultimate.

See also, *Über*

Bestie (noun)

A term usually used by girls to describe someone who is so close that they are actually better than a best friend. Someone who will be loyal, non-judgemental, forgiving, supportive, kind and dependable.

Until she meets a boy and drops you.

See also, *BFF, BFFL*

BF (noun)

Since this can mean boyfriend or best friend some conversations end up very *awky*. This is why it sometime pays to spend slightly longer typing and use the full word.

BFD (interjection)

Big fucking deal. Usually used sarcastically to show contempt for something or someone that others hold in high regard or at least respect.

> E.g.
> Friend: 'So Lily Allen's pregnant again. This time it's sextuplets!'
> You: 'BFD.'

BFF (noun)

Best friends forever; traditionally used by girls to indicate a very close relationship with someone and the intention that this will be a lifelong bond. However, BFF can also stand for big fat fuck. Ensure the person you are addressing is aware of your intended meaning.

> See also, *Bestie, BFFL*

BFFL (noun)

Best friends for life; similar to BFF but indicating slightly less commitment to the relationship. BFFL implies that your friendship will cease when one of you dies whereas BFF infers that it will continue into the afterlife or via some form of reincarnation.

Bible (adverb, interjection)

Adding this word to the end of a statement implies that what you have just said is the God's honest truth.

> E.g. 'I walked straight into the locker room and saw Zak getting off with Brandon. Bible!'

Bigorexia (noun)

Condition suffered by someone who spends excessive amounts of time at the gym and for whom muscles can never be large enough or sufficiently well-defined.

See also, *Body Nazi*

Bitch (noun)

(a) Degrading term for someone who performs tasks for another person.

(b) Degrading term for a male dominated by his girlfriend.

(c) Insulting term for a female who is malicious, aggressive, unreasonable, belligerent and usually insulting/ condescending towards other females behind their backs.

(d) Humorous term of affection for friends, male or female.

Bitchin' (adjective, verb)

(a) To excessively complain/whine/moan about something

(b) A way to describe something that was *awesome* or the action of having an *awesome* time.

E.g. 'Stop bitchin' about the buffet! That party was bitchin'.'

Bitch slap (noun, verb)

A powerful blow to the side of the face with the flat of the hand. The term can also be used to describe a humiliating defeat of an individual or a team.

E.g. 'Did you watch the game? Another bitch slap for Chelsea.'

Biz (adjective)

(a) To be occupied, e.g. 'I can't come over. I'm *batshit* biz.'

(b) Things that you have to do, e.g. 'Man, I got to get through a ton o' biz.'

Blah (noun)

(a) A feeling of apathy, complete and utter boredom or hopelessness, e.g. 'I failed my mocks, can't get a summer job or a girlfriend. Right now my life is just so blah.'

(b) Indicating confusion over what you actually feel or think. E.g. 'So I told him that I hated him and his stupid friends and his dumb band, but he was looking so buff and he grinned and . . . and . . . well . . . blah . . .'

(c) The words you hear when you parents are moaning about something you've done – or more usually, haven't done – e.g 'How many times do I have to tell you to blah, blah, blah, blah, blah, blah, blah . . .'

Bling/Bling-bling (noun)

Gaudy, sparkly jewellery, often encrusted with diamonds (fake or real) that falls into two categories.

(1) Looks cheap. Is cheap

(2) Looks cheap. Is expensive.

Bling is usually worn to give an impression of wealth. In reality the only impression it gives is one of complete lack of class. As a guide, the larger the piece, the smaller the wearer's self-esteem.

See also, *Chav*

Bling up (verb)

To accessorise with jewels, precious metals (real or fake) and sometimes fur, in order to attract attention, look expensive and impart a sense of glamour and desirability.

E.g.

Friend: 'Check out my blinged-up wheels; Swarovski encrusted badges, mother of pearl paint and gold-plated, twenty-inch rims.'

You: 'But it's a W-reg Corsa.'

Blinkage (noun)

The degree to which you've got your eyes closed in a photograph (usually a *selfie*). Too much blinkage and the photo will never make it to a social media site.

Blitzed (adjective)

The effect of excessive alcohol and/or drug consumption. Signs include incoherence, confusion and the sending of obscene texts to your ex.
    See also, *Hammered, Rekt, Wasted*

Blitzed out (adjective)

The state of being so completely drunk/drugged up that you can't recall (a) how you got into this state and (b) any of your subsequent actions – no matter how *cray cray* they were.

Blow (verb)

Something that is extremely disappointing or which is very poor quality.
    E.g. 'That new Adam Sandler film totally blows.'
    See also, *Suck/sucks*

Blow chunks (verb)

Something that is a complete and utter letdown and an unmitigated disaster.
    E.g. 'That new Rob Schneider film totally blows chunks.'
    See also, *Blow, Suck/sucks*

Blow it up (verb)

Description of an action or performance that exceeds all expectations and is taken to a whole new level.

E.g. 'Olly Murs so blew it up last night!' (NB, in reality this sentence would probably never be uttered).

Bodybag (adjective)

The opposite of *butters*; someone (usually female) who is said to have a beautiful face but the body of a deformed hippo. So called because the nicest thing to do with her body is to cover it with a bag.

See also, *Baggable, Butters, Fugly*

Body Nazi (noun)

Hardcore bodybuilder who spends all his/her spare time in the gym and looks contemptuously at anyone who doesn't.

Bone (verb)

To have sex with, but can also be used a nickname for trombone.

e.g.

You: 'The first violist said she liked how I played my bone and I ended up boning her.'

Friend: 'Yeah. Shoulda waited 'til after the concert though.'

Boner (noun)

An erection, but the term is more commonly used for an erection that happens at the most inappropriate, *awky* times; e.g. on the bus, standing at the front of the class during show-and-tell, during PE, when a friend sits on your lap, watching a Disney film.

See also, *Pop a stiffy, Road bone, Sympathy boner*

Boo (noun)

A boyfriend or girlfriend but a word that's being losing popularity to the more recent term *bae*.

Body Nazi

Boobage (adjective)

A general term for a woman's *chestal* area. Used when referring to breasts and/or cleavage.

E.g. 'Wow! Did you see Erika on that trampoline. That was some serious boobage action going on.'

The Book (noun)

What *fucktards* call Facebook.

E.g. 'I loved what you posted on the Book.'

Boom! (interjection)

Added to the conclusion of a sentence to emphasise the gravity, significance and sheer awesomeness of what has just been stated; an exclamation of joy.

NB, incorrect use of the word diminishes its significance and effect. And makes you look like a *tool*.

Appropriate usage:

'I just got off with Carly in the downstairs loo. Boom!'

'Boys' week in Ibiza booked. Boom!'

Inappropriate usage:

'I just found my other sock. Boom!'

'Double fried egg on toast. Boom!'

See also, *Booyah!, Booyakah!*

Booty call (noun, verb)

A late night phone call, text message, tweet etc., usually made by a male to a female with the sole intention of meeting up for sex. And by 'meeting up' I mean 'begging'. A booty call can be made to an existing partner, someone you know casually or, more usually, your ex.

Booyah!/Boo yah! (interjection)

A spoken exclamation mark used in a similar way to *Boom!* but can also mean '*In your face!*' or 'Hell, yeah!'
   See also, *Boom!, Booyaka!*

Booyaka!/booyakah! (interjection)

A variation of *booyah!*
   See also, *Boom!*

Boss (adjective)

Someone or something that is exceptionally *awesome*. Rarely, if ever, actually used to describe your workplace line manager.
   See also, *Beast, Epic, Prime*

Bounce (verb)

To leave somewhere quickly, usually to somewhere better. Bouncing from a party, for example, should be done quickly and discreetly. Saying your goodbyes just draws attention to yourself.
   See also, *Bail, Dip/dip out, Ghost/ghosting*

Bov (adjective)

A state of apathy; can refer to a situation in which you don't care about something/someone or one in which you lack motivation to do something. Contraction of the word 'bovvered'.
   E.g.
   Friend: 'The Steps reunion tour's been cancelled!'
   You: 'Me? Bov?'
Warning: this is not to be confused with the acronym BOV to describe either a very fat girl (belly over vagina) or the customary entrance fee for a house party (bottle of vodka).

Bovvered (adjective)

The same meaning as *bov* but used when you have the luxury of time and don't need to contract this word.

See also, *Bov*

Boyed (verb)

To be shamed or made fun of as a result of something bad happening to you. This could be the result of something as innocuous as tripping over, or something as disastrous as being mauled by an escaped puma.

E.g. 'I can't believe you fell for that scam and really believed you were heir to the fortune of a Nigerian prince! You were well and truly boyed!'

Boyfriend/girlfriend drop (verb)

Unexpectedly mentioning a significant other in a conversation, usually to deter over-affection on the part of someone you're finding either a bit creepy or too full-on.

E.g. 'So I'd been talking to this hot, long-haired guy in the coffee shop for ages when he suddenly girlfriend-dropped!'

Brainfart/Brain fart (noun)

This happens when your brain is suddenly flooded by the stupidity endorphin. There are usually three stages to a brainfart:
  (1) A momentary loss of attention coupled with a blank expression.
  (2) Saying something irrelevant or really dumb.
  (3) A feeling of overwhelming shame and embarrassment.
  E.g.
  You: 'You OK for five-a-side tonight?'
  Friend: 'I love you.'
  You: '*WTF*?!'

Friend: 'Sorry. I was miles away. Total brainfart!'
See also, *Mental hairball*

BRB (interjection)

Be right back; what to type when you have to temporarily leave any online conversation. It's the online equivalent of Arnie saying, 'I'll be back . . .' but without the drama and latent threat.
See also, *AFK, BRBx*

BRBx (interjection)

Be right back in X minutes . . . so if you planned to be away from the conversation for five minutes you'd type BRB5. NB, X is always approximate, so that five minutes might be any time from five minutes to never.

Breastimate (verb)

To judge the bust and cup size of a woman; a puerile game played by young teenage males.
   E.g.
   Young teenage boy one: 'Jeez! I breastimate she's 34DD'
   Young teenage boy two: 'No way, man! I breastimate 36C'
   Young teenage boy three: 'Dudes. That's a man. We're staring at *moobs!*'

Brill (adjective)

Brilliant in its widest sense i.e. it can be used to describe something or someone that is magnificent, intelligent, distinguished, talented, vivid or sparkling. NB, something can be both brill and *ill* at the same time.

Bro (noun)

A male friend. The *street* way to say buddy, mate, pal or chum.
   See also, *Bruv, Bruvva, Bud, Dude*

Bromance (noun)

A very close relationship between two men that leads to others
viewing them as a couple, but which does not involve romance or
anything like touching each other's bottoms.

Bruv (noun)

Abbreviated version of *bruvva* which can be used in many
contexts. For example, it is an acceptable form of address when
talking to both a close male friend or a complete stranger and is
equally appropriate when used in either a friendly or aggressive
manner.
   E.g. 'Alright bruv?' or 'Look at my girl again and I'll kill you,
bruv.'
   See also, *Bro, Bud, Dude*

Bruvva (noun)

See *bruv.*

BT dubs (interjection)

When you haven't the time or inclination to say 'by the way' you
can just use the acronym BTW . . . But hold on . . . the letter 'W'
is far too long to say out loud . . . Ah, I know, we can shorten it to
'dubs' instead.
   See also, *BTW*

BTW (interjection)

Short for 'by the way' when typing.
> E.g. 'I love that track "BTW" by RHCP.'
> See also, *BT dubs*

Bud (noun)

See *bro, bruv, dude*

Bud-in-law/buddy-in-law (noun)

Your friend's friend; a mutual friend.

Buff (adjective)

Usually, but not exclusively, used to describe boys or men who are good-looking and also muscular. Can also be used to describe someone who is a yellowish-beige colour.
> See also *Fit, Reem, Swole*

Bugly (adjective)

Short for butt ugly; Exceeded on the ugly ranking by *dugly* and *fugly*.
> See also, *Bodybag, Butters*

Built (adjective)

Someone really strong and muscly.
> See also, *Hench, Ripped, Swole*

Bumpin' (adjective)

A really cool event, usually a club night or party, that's in full swing
> See also, *Bangin', Lit, Poppin'*

Busted (verb)

(a) To be caught doing something you shouldn't or being discovered telling a lie.

E.g.

Friend: 'Yeah, I saw Busted play Wembley in March 2005.'

You: 'Liar! They split up in January that year. Busted!'

(b) Occasionally used to describe shooting a gun (busting a cap) but more commonly referring to punching or hitting someone really, really hard.

E.g.

Friend: 'He said he was gonna bust a cap in my ass so I busted his face.'

You: 'I can tell you don't get on with your grandfather.'

Butt dial/buttdial (noun, verb)

Accidentally phoning or texting someone (usually the last person you made contact with) when your phone is in your pocket. The result is a very confused person responding to your trousers.

Butters (adjective)

Term of abuse for someone considered ugly. Usually (but not exclusively) used to describe women and a corruption of the phrase 'but her'.

E.g. 'Man, she has a stokin' hot body but her face looks like it caught on fire and they put it out with a fork.'

See also, *Baggable, Fugly*

Cakin' (verb)

Excessive flirting or spending far too long on the phone with a boy/girl. Any phone call that ends with the conversation 'You hang up first', 'No, *you* hang up' is *absofuckinglutely* a cakin' call.

Cankle (noun)

The part of the body where someone's calves morph seamlessly into their ankles to form one undefined fleshy mass. Common among the overweight but instantly cured by wearing boots.

Caraoke (noun)

To sing along to music in the car, usually with complete disregard to the song's original pitch, tempo or volume. Or lyrics.
E.g.
Friend: 'Hey! Bette Midler. "Wind Beneath my Wings"! Crank it up. Time for some caraoke!'
You: 'Shut the fuck up.'

Catfish (noun, verb)

Somebody with a fake personality who uses social media in order to lure a victim into some sort of relationship. Term derives from the documentary film *Catfish* which later became an MTV series.

E.g. 'That girl was totally catfished when she finally met that fugly guy from the chat room! He wasn't a personal trainer to the stars! He lives at home with his mum and spends all day playing *Warhammer.'*

CBA (interjection)

Can't be arsed. When you're in a state of *blah* and have absolutely no inclination to do anything. Often used in response to a question where you don't want to give your real reason for declining an invitation.

E.g.

Friend: 'Boyz nite! Jez, Mez, Fez, Les, Sol and Lol. Beers. Laser tag. Amy's leaving do. Deano's eighteenth, Kyle's twenty-first. Clubbing then meet with Jenna's crew for rave. You in?

You: 'CBA.'

See also, *Blah, CBF, Ceebs, Meh*

CBF (interjection)

Can't be fucked. Like *CBA* but when you want to indicate an even greater state of apathy.

CCL (noun)

It's not that often that you'll need to reference a 'crazy cat lady' in a text or email etc., but if you ever do, this is the acronym to use.

Ceebs (interjection)

Short form – and a more polite way – of saying *CBF*.

See also, *CBA*

Cellfish (adjective)

The term given to someone who uses their mobile phone in a rude and selfish manner i.e. while someone is talking to them, or making calls in a public place where its use is detrimental to the ambience.

E.g. 'And she was even sexting during her granny's funeral. How cellfish!'

Chav (noun)

Although not as popular nowadays this insult is still applied to someone who suffers from in-bred stupidity and congenital ugliness. The chav is someone who possesses the good looks and charm of Wayne Rooney, is obsessed with designer clothes (usually fake) and who has little or no understanding of the words 'taste' or 'style'. Chavs can be found loitering outside fast-food outlets and their favourite pastimes are aggression, smoking, drinking cheap lager, vandalism, spitting and dreaming of being famous.

Chavette (noun)

Female *chav*. As above but also characterised by having hair scraped back so tight that the only facial expression possible is disappointment, a T-shirt that says 'Slut' worn without any sense of irony, hoop earrings so large you could throw a basketball through them and tight trousers that display a nylon thong and a butt-crack that would put most builders to shame. Chavettes are usually parents at fourteen and end up on the Jeremy Kyle show two years later.

Chaviot (noun)

What chavs drive. Usually small hatchbacks that are unroadworthy, untaxed and uninsured, held together by filler and fibreglass. Typically driven like they are stolen . . . because they usually are.

Chestal, chestal area (noun)

Describing the chest area of a man or a woman.
 See also, *Boobage, Chestacular, Chestalicious*

Chestacular (adjective)

Evocative way of describing impressively large women's breasts, this term is almost exclusively used by thirteen-year-old boys.

Chestne (noun)

Having acne on your upper chest. Less commonly known as known as *Breastme*.
 See also, *Assne, Bacne/backne, Rackne*

Chill/Chillin' (noun, verb)

(a) To relax/calm down, e.g. 'So what if that huge zit's erupted on your nose? I'm sure she won't notice. Just chill.'
(b) To hang out, e.g. 'I'm jus' chillin' with my peeps.'
(c) To stop doing something, e.g. 'Just chill the fucking track will ya? I hate Matt Cardle.'
(d) Someone who is very cool, e.g. 'With that retro jacket and glasses that new girl looks so chill.'
(e) Something that's cool, e.g. 'iPhone 7? That's super chill!'
(f) It's OK, e.g. 'So you fancy James Corden? That's chill.'

Chillax (adjective)

A term that severely over-used to the point of causing intense irritation, this combination of 'chill' and 'relax' is likely to result in the speaker being punched for saying it. This is ironic since the word is used as an instruction to tell someone to calm down.

Chill pill/chillpill (noun)

Imaginary medication to reduce mental stress and help you relax/ calm down.

E.g. 'So you've got a girl preggers and her old man's in the Yakuza? Stop worrying and just take a chill pill.'

Chirpsin' (verb)

The act of gently flirting with someone; not as aggressive as *hitting on* them.

E.g.

You: 'I think my phone must be broken. It doesn't have your number in it.'

Girl: 'You chirpsin' wi'me?'

Chirpsinator (noun)

Someone flirtatious and very, very smooth with the ladies. Or who thinks he is.

See also, *Playa, Player*

Chub (noun)

A semi-boner.

E.g. 'That Kylie Jenner bikini photo. Wow! Chub *city*!'

Church (adverb, interjection)

The equivalent and more streetwise way of saying 'Amen!' Responding to a statement with this word means you agree wholeheartedly with what's just been said.

See also, *Totz me goats*

City (adjective)

A suffix used for emphasis to convey 'an excessive amount of'.

E.g. 'Wow. Look at those fit guys. It's like *buff* city' or 'That club might as well be renamed *Dork* City.'

Clean (adjective)

Term used to describe something that is new, fine and stylish, and by inference, highly desirable.

E.g. 'That red metal flake BMW convertible that just rolled by? Mmmm . . . clean.'

See also, *Tight*

Clown car it (verb)

When there are more people in a car than seat belts and as a consequence, passengers are sitting on laps, lying across people, poking out of windows etc.

E.g. 'There's seven of us and just my mum's car. I guess we'll have to clown-car it.'

Cocoon (verb)

To regularly stay at home watching TV or using the computer rather than socialising with people face to face.

Commando (adjective)

Going commando is the state of not wearing any underwear. There's a certain allure when girls use the term, however when boys use it the usual response is 'Eww!'

See also, *Freeballing*

Confusticated (adjective)

When you're confused and frustrated simultaneously. Can apply to a multitude of issues ranging from trying to find your way out of a car park to body dysmorphia.

Confuzzled (adjective)

When you're confused and puzzled simultaneously. i.e the state of not knowing *WTF* is going on.
  See also, *Confuzzling*

Confuzzling (adjective)

Epic bewilderment.
  See also, *Confuzzled*

Convo (noun)

Short for conversation. Can apply to spoken dialogue but more usually texting.

Convo 180 (noun)

When a conversation is completely (and usually unexpectedly) turned around.
  E.g. 'So I was telling Alex that we needed to take a break. Next thing I know, she's dumping *me*. Talk about a convo 180!'

Cool (adjective)

The go-to word when you can't think of any way to describe something or respond to a question or comment; ubiquitous way of referring to anything that is at least one of the following: awesome, astounding, amazing, astonishing, delightful or splendid. 'Cool' is one of the few slang words that never really goes out of style and can be used in context with people, animals and inanimate objects (although describing broccoli or toilet paper as cool might be stretching plausibility).

See also *Amazeballs, Chill, Dope, Fly, Hip, Kickass, Killer, Neat, Phunky, Savage, Shiny, Swag*

Cool beans! (interjection)

An alternative, but slightly less cool way of saying 'Cool', usually used as an expression of approval or agreement.

E.g.

Friend: 'I got those Pharrell tickets.'

You: 'Cool beans!'

See also, *Neat beets!*

Coolify (verb)

The process of making yourself or a friend more fashionable and socially acceptable. This is usually achieved by changing your/their haircut, clothes and music; the main ways teens judge their peers.

Coolio (adjective)

An alternate way of saying *cool;* usually said by those trying to sound ironic.

Coolio hoolio (adjective)

Another way of saying the word cool. NB, using it is another way of getting your friends to view you as an *A-hole.*

Cool story, bro (interjection)

Sarcastic response when someone says something that you really don't give a shit about. Another way of saying *whatevs.*

E.g.

Friend: 'So my mum and dad suddenly drop three bombs on me. First, they tell me I'm adopted, then my dad says he's going to become a woman and then my mum says she's leaving my dad for my uncle.'

You: 'Cool story, bro.'

Cosplay (noun, verb)

Contraction of 'costume play'; dressing up and pretending to be a fictional character in order to fill a void in your sad life. Less sexual fantasy and more *batshit* weird.

See also, *Fanboy/fanboi (and fangirl)*

Couch gold (noun)

Money found down the back of a sofa.

E.g. 'I couldn't afford to go to the pub but then I decided to turn over all the cushions and found about two pounds in couch gold. Still wasn't enough.'

Craction (noun)

The state (usually unintentional) of displaying your butt crack while wearing low-cut jeans or trousers.

E.g. 'I wanted to wear my new low-rise jeans with my crop top but when I looked in the mirror there was just a little too much craction going on.'

Craptacular (adjective)

A spectacularly high level of crappiness.

See also, *Craptastic*

Craptastic (adjective)

(a) The highest degree of crappiness that can ever be attained, e.g. 'Angie's parents have split up and neither wants custody of her. That's so craptastic.'

Couch Gold

(b) Something so bad, it's almost good, e.g. 'Have you seen
    Zombie Strippers? It's craptastic!'
See also, *Craptacular*

Craptop (adjective, noun)

Derogatory name for any laptop not made by Apple. A putdown
that's at best mildly amusing but which is thought to be the
height of sophisticated wit by Apple *fanboys*.

Cray (adjective)

Not the slang word for crayfish or crayons (although it could
be), this is an abbreviated version of crazy. Often repeated for
emphasis.
    E.g. 'Hey, bro. You can't say that dude is cray cray! You have to
say he suffers from mental health problems!'

Crazified (adjective)

A quick way of describing someone who's acting crazy.

Credz (noun)

Short form of the word 'credit' which can be used in two ways:
    (a) Acknowledging someone's input or action, e.g. 'I look like I
        lost twenty pounds? Credz to JoJo for her Photoshop skills!'
    (b) Reference to a monetary amount, usually in context with
        mobile phone usage, e.g. 'Can you call her? I'm outta credz.'

Creep (noun)

    (a) Someone unpleasant, bothersome, undesirable or weird –
        with little understanding of, or interest in, accepted social
        boundaries.
    (b) Anyone a girl isn't interested in.

Creepellant/creepelent (adjective)

Someone who is so creepy that their creepiness actually makes you feel physically nauseous and revolted.

E.g. 'That guy who jumped out of the bushes wearing just a giant nappy . . . he was so creepellant I just wanted to vom!'

Creeperazzi (noun)

Someone who takes photos (usually embarrassing, compromising or just not particularly flattering) of others without their knowledge which, to their horror, end up on social media sites.

Creep out (verb)

To disturb or bother someone and generally make them feel uncomfortable. Creeping out can take many forms including scouring Facebook to glean personal information, staring at someone or stealing their underwear.

Crew (noun)

A *tight* group of friends
    See also, *Fam, Mains, Peeps, Squad*

Crib (noun)

Your house or home. Only to be used if you fall into one of these categories:
    (a) You're trapped in the year 2004.
    (b) You're in a rap band.
    (c) You want people to think you're a grade-A *douche*.

Cringe (noun, verb)

The act of, or the feeling associated with, someone doing something unbelievably embarrassing.

E.g. ' So Taylor emailed his love poem to Jen but accidentally sent it to the whole class. It was so cringe!'
    See also, *Awkfest, Awky, Cringeworthy*

Cringeworthy (adjective)

Used to describe any action that is worthy of a cringe.
    See also *Cringe, Awkfest, Awky*

Cropduster (noun)

Someone who farts while walking, running or cycling.
    See also, *Dusted*

Crunk (adjective)

When you're extremely intoxicated and likely to do something particularly reckless. Derived from the words 'crazy' and 'drunk' and a more hip way of saying *wasted* and a more polite way of saying *shitfaced*.
    See also, *Turnt*

Cuddle buds/cuddle buddy (noun)

Those in a *cuddleship*; a platonic relationship between two close friends, one of whom is desperately wishing for something more.

Cuddleship (noun)

A relationship that is more about physical embracing and hugging rather than sexual activity.
    E.g.
    Friend: 'Jon and Em? Are they an item?
    You: 'Nah. It's just a cuddleship'
    Friend: 'Ohh . . . They're cuddle buds'.

Cult of Mac (noun)

Someone who belongs to this fictitious cult is obsessed with Apple products to the point that they'd sacrifice their children (if they had any) to ensure they have the latest piece of tech with a partially eaten fruit logo on it. They will queue all night to ensure they're first to buy a new product which has superficial changes over the last one they also queued all night for.

See also, *Craptop, Fanboi, Fanboy*

Cumberbitch (noun)

A female fan obsessed with the actor Benedict Cumberbatch because of his sultry good looks, tousled hair and, oh yes, acting ability. If a Cumberbitch meets the subject of her fixation she will want to do two things: (a) have sex, (b) polish his cheekbones.

Cuool (adjective)

Someone who is both cute and cool.

Cuz (noun)

A term that can be used to describe your biological cousin or a friend.

E.g.

Friend: Hey, cuz. What's the name for the child of my aunt's child?'

You: 'Cuz, that'll be your first cuz once removed.'

Da bomb (adjective)

Still used but a really, really, really passé way of saying something is the best, *cool* or *awesome*. Unless you're using it with a sense of irony, like *crib,* think twice (then think again) before using this word.

DAF (adjective)

Drunk as fuck.
　See also, *Crunk, Lit, Hammered, Sauced, Trashed, Turnt, Wasted*

Dank (adjective)

Something *cool, awesome* or *fresh.*

Dap/daps (noun)

A greeting where you bump fists or a far more complex combination of moves which involves an intricate sequence of palm slapping, back of hand slapping, wrist grabbing and fist bumping.
　E.g 'Dude. Dap me up!'

Date bail (verb)

To abandon a date early, usually as a result of a friend making a pre-arranged *bail-out call* to you.

E.g. 'Joanna offered to date-bail me next Friday when Dane's taking me to Nandos.'

See also, *Bail-out call*

Dawg (noun)

Your close friend or colleague. Someone who's more *street* than a *dude*. Exclusively used by males and usually preceded by the word *waddup* or *wassup*.

Dayam/dayum (interjection)

The two syllables in this word make it a stronger version of 'damn' as an expression of anger or wonder.

E.g. 'Dayam! That girl is hott.'

Dead (adjective)

(a) Something that is sooo hilariously funny that you almost killed yourself laughing, e.g. 'That scene in *Bridesmaids* when she shits in the sink. Dead!'

(b) A place or event that has completely lost its charm or any appeal, e.g. 'When the only bottle left was Diet 7 Up I knew that party was dead.'

(c) An indication someone is in serious trouble with a person in authority, e.g. 'If your manager sees you jacking the till, you're so dead!'

Dealio (noun)

A more *street* way of saying 'deal', referring to an arrangement or transaction rather than distributing playing cards. Can also be used as a greeting, a way of saying, 'Hello. What is going on here?'

Dece (adjective)

A cooler and faster way of saying 'decent' but not limited to describing someone who is honest, caring, ethical or polite. This term is just as relevant when used to describe inanimate objects.
    E.g. 'That KFC Mighty Bucket was well dece.'

Deck (verb)

To deck someone is to hit them so hard that they fall to the ground and/or are knocked unconscious.
    E.g. 'As soon as that hipster said he wasn't a barista, he was a "coffee ninja" I just knew I had to deck him.'

Deck it/decking it (verb)

To accidentally trip and fall over; usually in a public place for maximum embarrassment.
    See also, *Face plant*

Decompress (verb)

To relax and de-stress. To wind down after a really shitty day.

Deep (adjective)

Quick way of indicating to someone that their comment is harsh or cruel (even though it may be a hundred per cent accurate).
    E.g.
    Friend: 'Carla's so dumb that blondes tell jokes about her.'
    You: 'Deep.'

Deets (noun)

A term for details or information, often used to refer to gossip.
    E.g. 'So Maz and Shaz started hangin' and ended up bangin'? Gimme the sweet deets!'

Def/defs/deffo/defo (adverb)

Certainly, sure, without a doubt. This term has the advantage of not having to remember whether the full word is spelled definitely, definitly, definately or definatly – or any other variation – plus it's cooler to say.

See also, *Fo' sho*

Deface (verb)

Alternative but less popular term for *De-friend* or *Unfriend*.

De-friend (verb)

To remove one of your contacts from Facebook who you find boring, annoying, embarrassing, too self-promoting – or because their comments are just predictable or dumb rather than funny.

See also, *Deface, Unfriend*

Deligious (adjective)

As many teenagers know, pizza instantly transcends the gulf between famine and fulfilment and the effect can become an almost spiritual experience. Use this term when referring to something so tasty, refreshing or delicious that consuming it is almost a religious experience.

Derp (adjective, noun, verb)

A word used to describe something incredibly stupid, awkward, random or weird. Examples might include putting a wasp's nest down your trousers, having a tattoo of your teacher inked across your back along with the slogan, 'Live to learn' or adopting the fashion sensibilities of Effie Trinket.

- As an adjective: 'Trust him to do something so derpy!'
- As a noun: 'Jesus. That guy's a real derp!'
- As a verb: 'He's going to be derping tonight, I just know it.'

A less popular usage is to use the word as a response when someone asks you a question or makes a statement and you can't think of anything at all to say in return.

E.g.

Parent: 'If it wasn't you then who was it then who crashed my car into next door's ornamental fish pond?'

You: ' . . . derp.'

Derpzilla (noun)

Someone whose actions are stupid or clumsy.

See also, *Derp*

Derpzoid (noun)

See *derpzilla*

Designated texter (noun)

A car passenger who's been given the honour/responsibility to respond to all texts received by the driver while the car is in motion.

Devo'd (adjective)

Absolutely gutted; distraught. Used when you're so traumatised you can't even bring yourself to say the whole of 'devastated'.

DGAF (interjection)

See *IDGAF*

DIAF (interjection)

Die in a fire. An indication to someone that their presence on this planet is no longer required; a more aggressive comeback than *FOAD*. Can also mean 'die in a fridge', to be said to someone you dislike enough to wish them a slow suffocation, but not enough that you wish them a painful death being combusted at up to 600 degrees C.

Other variations are as follows:

DIACF: die in a car fire/die in a chemical fire.

DIAFF: die in a fucking fire.

DIAGF: die in a grease fire.

DIAFGF: die in a fucking grease fire.

See also, *FOAD, FOADAB, FOAGDIAF*

Dick around (verb)

To spend time being unproductive; to fool around or be lazy.

Dickwad (noun)

The successor to the insult formerly known as dickhead.

See also, *A-hole*

DILF (noun)

Dad I'd like to fuck. A really hot father; the male equivalent of a *MILF*. Most men over forty-five think they fall into this category. They absolutely do not.

Dip/dip out (verb)

To leave suddenly or to run away from something.

E.g. 'And when the DJ put on Coldplay I knew it was time to dip.'

See also, *Bail, Bounce, Ghost, Ghosting*

Dipshit (noun)

Another way of describing a *dickwad* or a *dumbtard*.

Dis/diss/dissed (adjective, verb)

To disrespect someone i.e. treat them with condescension and contempt usually by ignoring or insulting them.

E.g.

You: 'Your new hoody makes a statement. It says, "I look like a *tool*."'

Friend: 'You dissin' me?'

See also, *Par/parred*

Docious (adjective)

Anything that is super *awesome/über* cool. Far easier than having to type 'Supercalifragilisticexpialidocious' – and leaves you plenty of characters in a text message to use for even more crass and absurd slang.

Dogg (noun)

Close friend or companion.

See also, *Homeboy, Homie*

Dope (adjective)

The cool way to say cool.

See also *Amazeballs, Cool, Fly, Hip, Kickass, Killer, Phunky, Savage, Swag*

Dork (noun)

Someone (usually a male) who is socially awkward but who has an individual style and sense of humour that no one really gets and who may also have odd interests such as *Warcraft*, anime, *Lord of the Rings*, programming, juggling, *Star Wars* and keeping amphibians.

Their flouting of traditional teenage social norms can make them appear *cool*.
  See also, *Dweeb, Geek, Neek, Nerd*

Dorky (adjective)

The practice of acting like a *dork*.
  See also, *Adorkable*

Douche (noun)

An individual whose character traits include unpleasantness, obnoxiousness and stupidity and therefore an apt comparison with a product designed to sanitise and cleanse vaginas.
Can also be used in the longer form, *douchebag*.
  See also, *A-hole, Asshole, Tool, Tool bag*

Down (adjective)

To be aware of what's *on trend*; what used to be known as being 'with it' or 'in the know' about something.
  E.g. 'Girls Aloud. Atomic Kitten. Destiny's Child. Sure. I'm down when it comes to hot bands.'

Do you even lift? (interjection)

A patronising remark questioning physical fitness/ability – or a fitness regime. Doesn't have to be used in reference to bodybuilding.

Drink-dial/Drunkdial (noun, verb)

  (a) Calling someone when you are *hammered* (usually between 1 a.m. and 3.30 a.m.) and trying to embark on a conversation that is either embarrassing or bizarre which includes you stating how much you've already drunk and then proceeding to get quite emotional. Recipients of drunk-dials are usually ex-partners or people you have a grudge against while discussions usually include getting back together or violent threats.

(b) An excuse for a phone call that you now horribly regret.

Drop the F-bomb (interjection)

To say 'fuck' when you really shouldn't.

E.g.

You: 'I couldn't believe when Sarah dropped that F-bomb during holy communion!'

Friend: 'But it was in context, right?'

Dude (interjection, noun)

Universal greeting for any male friend. Usually followed by the question *'Zup?'*

See also, *Bro, Bruv, Bud*

Dugly (adjective)

Short for dog ugly. Someone uglier than *bugly* but not as ugly as *fugly.*

See also, *Bodybag, Butters*

Duh! (interjection)

A short and more polite way of saying, 'Of course I know that, you moronic *fucktard.'*

Dumbtard (noun)

A particularly stupid person who demonstrates the qualities of someone who is both a dumbass and educationally retarded.

See also, *Fucktard*

Dusted (verb)

To be dusted is to fall victim to someone's farts as they pass by you.

　　See also, *Cropduster*

Dweeb (noun)

Dork meets *nerd*; a loser.

Dweet (noun, verb)

The act of tweeting while drunk or the drunken tweet itself.
　　E.g.
　　You: 'Thdg5 hfs4££ hjkGD98h6% gdbxwl'
　　Friend: *'Whatever.'*
　　See also, *Drunk-dial/drunkdial, Dwext*

Dwext (noun, verb)

The act of texting while drunk or the drunken text message itself. Dwexts usually fall into two categories:
　　(a) A random and senseless collection of characters, numerals, symbols or emojis.
　　(b) A message saying you're on your way over for a quickie . . . accidentally sent to your mum.
　　See also, *Drunk-dial/drunkdial, Dweet*

Dusted – by a Cropduster

Earjack (verb)

To eavesdrop on a private conversation in the hope of learning something to your advantage.

E.g. 'Shazza totally earjacked me phoning Dazza. Now she knows I'm two-timing Gazza!'

See also, *Goss, Juicy goss*

Earworm (noun)

A catchy song that gets stuck in your head, keeps repeating itself and is almost impossible to forget. Usually one you hate.

Eighthead, Eight head (noun)

Someone with a huge forehead, or the huge forehead itself, i.e. it's twice the size of two normal foreheads.

Emosh (adjective)

To be in a very emotional state. Usually proceeded by the word *totes.*

Ends (noun)

Money.

See also, *Bank, Mad stacks, Peas*

Endz (noun)

Your street or immediate neighbourhood.
  See also, *Yard*

Emoji (noun)

Small cartoons you insert in texts so you appear creative, funny or whimsical, which take longer to find and insert than just typing the actual words.

Emoticon (noun)

Ancient practice of representing facial expressions using various combinations of keyboard characters. What parents call *emojis*.

Epic (adjective)

Meaning incredible or impressive but usually overused in epic proportions, e.g. when used as prefix before words like car, meal, album, gig, trousers, haircut, hangover and fart. Its inappropriate use in these situations can be considered an *epic fail*.

Epic fail (adjective)

See *epic*

Eye bogies/eye noogies (noun)

Small sticky or crusty residue that collects in the corner of your eye when you're asleep and which is oh-so-fulfilling to scratch out when you wake up.

Fabulise (verb)

To improve something; usually used in context with fashion or personal appearance.

Facebook ho' (noun)

Someone (usually female) who posts revealing photographs of themselves on Facebook in a desperate attempt to gain attention/ feel wanted.

Facebook minute (noun)

A difficult to define, and uncertain, length of time that elapses between someone saying they're just going to check their Facebook messages and then actually completing this action.

E.g.

You: 'Where the hell's Debz?'

Friend: 'She's just checking her status. She'll be back in a Facebook minute.'

You: 'That was two hours ago.'

Facebook official (adjective)

When a romantic relationship has been legitimised and reference is made on the couples' Facebook profiles. NB, a status referring to the relationship might include the abbreviation FBO.

E.g.
Friend: 'So Pol and A. J. are really an item?'
You: 'Seems like it. It's Facebook official.'

Facejack (verb)

To change someone's personal details or status when they leave their Facebook profile unattended. This is usually done to cause embarrassment or humiliation rather than out of any real vindictiveness.

E.g. 'I didn't realise I'd been facejacked until people started asking if I really wanted to have Rolf Harris's babies.'

Face palm (verb)

The action of pressing your palm against your face because you find something so *awky* or embarrassing. E.g. 'And when she got up on the desk and started twerking all I could do was face palm.'

Face plant (noun, verb)

To fall and hit the ground face first to the absolute amusement of any onlookers. This usually happens as a result of skateboarding, cycling, or anything that involves running or Jägerbombs.

See also *deck it/decking it*

Fake (adjective, noun)

Apart from meaning something that's not genuine or authentic (like *bling*, designer clothes, tattoos, hair extensions, IDs, nails or breasts) the term is more commonly used to describe a person:
  (a) Someone who acts cool but obviously isn't.
  (b) Someone who conceals or alters an aspect of their own personality because they want to be popular.
  (c) Someone who pretends to be your friend just for his or her personal gain.

Face Palm

NB, the word is often followed by the phrase 'as shit'.
  See also, *Begfriend/beg friend, Poser, Wannabe*

Fairs (interjection)

An indication that after due consideration you tend to agree with a statement or remark. Short form of 'fair enough'.

Faded (adjective)

Extremely impaired by alcohol or drugs but not quite *wasted.*
  See also, *Crunk, Hammered, Lit, Sauced, Trashed, Turnt*

Fam (noun)

This can refer to your biological family but more commonly it refers to a group of close friends you trust.
  E.g. 'My fam always has my back' or 'I'm spending Christmas back with my fam.'
  See also, *Main/mains, Peeps, Squad*

Fanboy/fanboi (and fangirl) (noun)

Derogative name for someone who's more than just a fan; someone who's obsessively and hopelessly devoted to something (usually a manufacturer, a product or a game, film or TV franchise involving science fiction, boy magicians, vampires or Hollow Earth) regardless of any deficiencies in or downsides to the subject of their affections. Fanboys treat all critics as *haters.*
  See also, *Cosplay*

Fanfic (noun)

Short for fanfiction; a story or script that uses characters, settings, and/or situations of an established TV series or film that's written by obsessive fans who genuinely think they can create something at least on a par with the originators. They can't.

See also, *Fanboy/fanboi (and fangirl)*

Fasterbate/fasturbate (verb)

The act of masturbating quickly to avoid detection by a parent, a roommate or the sales assistant who's looking after the changing rooms.

Fatfinger (verb)

To mis-type something, usually used in context with inputting a password or email address.

You: 'I didn't get that email from you.'

Friend: 'Got a bounce back. Sorry. Must have fatfingered the *addy.*'

Fauxpology (noun)

A token apology made without any sincerity just to bring an argument or accusation to a close without any admittance of blame or guilt.

See also, *Sor-ree!*

F-bomb (noun)

Euphemism for 'fuck'.

See also, *Drop the F-bomb*

Feels (noun)

A wave of intense, overwhelming emotion usually reserved for something rather than someone.

E.g. 'Every time I watch that scene where Dobby dies I get so many feels.'

'Fess, 'fess up (verb)

To admit guilt.

E.g. 'Fess up man! It's not funny. Where'd you hide my pre-shave Sandalwood balm and moisturiser?'

Fetch (adjective)

Cool or *awesome*. Originated in *Mean Girls* but still in use. The usual response is, 'Like, totally.'

Fierce (adjective)

Something fabulous or eye-catching; usually used in connection with fashion.

E.g. 'Girl, even though those Louboutins are knock-off you still look fierce!'

Filthy (adjective)

Can mean someone extremely talented or phenomenally *cool*.

E.g.

You: 'Did you see Frankie Boyle on TV. He was filthy!'

Friend: 'Do you mean he was awesome or crude?'

You: 'Yes.'

Finished (adjective)

Something that's completely and absolutely over and done with. Usually refers to a relationship but can also be used in context with the end of a long-running TV series or a young adult film franchise.

E.g.

You: 'You still seeing Felicia?'

Friend: 'No, man. We finished after *Hunger Games* finished.'

First world problems (noun)

Any issue which seems of paramount importance with huge consequences, but at the end of the day, is something that really just deserves a '*Meh.*'

E.g.

Friend: 'Should I get the new iPhone in space-grey or rose-gold? I've been going mental trying to make a decision!'

You: 'First world problem. . .'

Friend: '. . . or silver . . .'

Fit (adjective)

Extremely good-looking; can describe someone's general appearance without necessarily referring to their muscle definition. The British version of calling someone *buff* or *hot*.

See also, *Hott, Peng, Reem, Swole*

Flabdomen (noun)

An excess of fat on your torso.

E.g. 'I need to work out more. I'm developing quite a flabdomen.'

Flame (verb)

The act of posting hostile or offensive remarks on social media in order to insult and intimidate someone. Often viewed as a form of cyberbullying or abuse, the people posting flames are known as flamers**.** An alternative term is *fucktard.*

Flexin' (verb)

Showing off or gloating; can refer to personal achievements or material goods.

E.g. 'Did you see Deano flexin' his Air Max 90s? What a tool!'

See also, *No flex zone*

Flirtarded (adjective)

Someone who fails to recognise the signs of flirtation no matter how obvious these might be.

E.g. 'Dude. She was winking, blowing kisses, waggling her tongue while looking right at you and you never reacted once. You are so flirtarded!'

Flirtationship (noun)

A relationship that's more than just friendship but less than a romantic relationship.

A flirtationship can develop into a relationship though, sometimes via a *cuddleship*.

Fly (adjective)

See *Awesome, Cool, Hip, Kickass*

FML (interjecton)

Fuck my life. An exclamation made after notifying friends of something that happened to you that's unbelievably annoying, but more usually something so tragic or horrific that it will either affect your social standing or cause you never to show your face again. Or both.

E.g. 'My dad caught me NIFOC. What made it worse was that I was watching *Pocohontas*! FML.' or 'Some guy serving me at Burger King today kept addressing me as "sir". Couldn't he tell I have boobs? FML!'

FOAD (interjection)

Fuck off and die. A way of expressing extreme hatred towards someone or something.

See also, *FOADAB, FOAGDIAF*

66

FOADAB (interjection)

Fuck off and die and burn. When FOAD really doesn't express the strength of your feelings.

See also, *FOAD, FOAGDIAF*

FOAF (noun)

Friend of a friend. A way of telling a story about someone who did something unbelievably cringeworthy and embarrassing, while pretending it's not about you.

FOAGDIAF (interjection)

Fuck off and go die in a fire.

See also, *FOAD, FOADAB*

FoCo (noun)

Who'd have thought there'd be a need for a slang word for Food Court?

E.g.
Friend: 'Hey, mofo!'
You: 'Yo!'
Friend: FoCo?'
You: 'Fo' sho!'

FOH (interjection)

Fuck outta here; a shortened way of saying, 'I'm getting the fuck outta here,' or, 'Let's get the fuck outta here.'

E.g. 'Hey, mister. I can't be *arsed* with this job interview anymore. I'm FOH.'

FOMO (interjection)

Fear of missing out is perhaps the greatest fear a teenager will suffer. Untold stress and psychological trauma often accompany the fear that you're missing out on a great time or social event somewhere, and that everyone is having such a brilliant time without you.

E.g. 'I've got a migraine, flu and chronic diarrhoea but my FOMO is so max, I've got to go to Bestival.'

Foobs (noun)

Fake breasts.

Fo' real/for real (interjection)

Can be used:

(a) As a question, e.g. meaning 'Are you serious?'
(b) As a statement, e.g. meaning 'Most definitely!'
E.g.
Girlfriend: 'I'm dumping you.'
You: 'Fo' real?'
Girlfriend: 'Fo' real!'
See also, *Forilla*

Forilla/fo rilla (interjection)

If saying or asking 'fo' real?' doesn't sound *street* enough fo' you, then use this variation (if you must).

See also, *Fo' real/for real*

Fo' sho (interjection)

Of course, certainly, most definitely.

See also, *Def/defs/deffo/defo*

Freak out (verb)

To behave in a hyperactive, crazy, or manic way. While this state can be triggered by something good happening, the chances are that it'll be due to something very bad. NB, freaking out is not as intense (or violent) as *losing your shit*.

Freeballing (verb)

The process of going round without underwear (used for males).
See also, *Commando*

Frenchie/frenchy (verb)

See *spit swap, suck face*

Frenemy (noun)

Someone who likes you only because the relationship is beneficial to them, but who is apt to turn against you, undermine you or use you in some way. This term can also be used for someone you don't like or trust but who you treat as a friend in order to avoid conflict/friction.
See also, *Beg friend*

Fresh (adjective)

Something that's recognised as being *cool, on trend* or just generally of good quality.

Friended (verb)

The action of adding someone as a friend on Facebook.

Friending (verb)

The act of sending Facebook friend requests.

Friending spree (verb)

When you go *batshit* crazy and send a whole bunch of Facebook friend requests out because you're drunk or because you value quantity over quality.

E.g.
Friend: 'Wow! That chestacular hottie just friended me!'
You: 'And everyone else at the party . . . she was on a friending spree.'

Friendjack/friend jack (verb)

When you introduce someone to a social group and they end up being better friends with the group than you were – sometimes phasing you out completely.

E.g. 'It was me who introduced Karly to our group. Next thing I know she's everyone's BFF and they ignore me. She friendjacked the shit out of me!'

Friends with benefits (noun)

See *FWB*

Friendzone (noun, verb)

The metaphorical limbo-land where guys end up after unsuccessfully trying to date a girl. Your arrival in the friendzone is often announced by these words: 'You're such a good friend it would be so weird to date you'. Once in the friendzone it's *game over.* There is absolutely no way back from here. You automatically become an asexual being and you have to endure a long and frustrated period of suffering as you watch your would-be girlfriend go out with a procession of unsuitable guys, until she ends up in a serious relationship and you have to meet and be nice to her boyfriend when all you want to do is kill or severely maim him.

Can also be used as a verb, e.g. 'I really fancied Kimberly so I made my play. Next thing I know, I've been friendzoned!'

Frutal (adjective)

Something that is fucking brutal, i.e. something godawfully bad. NB, this has nothing to do with Frutal, a municipality in the west of the Brazilian state of Minas Gerais.

E.g.

Friend: 'When I was in Brazil I got stabbed and left for dead by these two muggers.'

You: 'No way! Where were you staying?'

Friend: 'Frutal.'

You: 'Frutal!'

FTW! (interjection)

(a) For the win! A way of adding emphasis to the end of a post or a message. The term can be used to signify encouragement to succeed in an action or to denote a surprising level of enthusiasm for something quite mundane.

E.g. 'Yay! Chocolate and raspberry cupcakes. FTW!'

(b) What the fuck! In this interpretation the intentional backwards spelling indicates an even greater state of shock, confusion or bewilderment.

E.g. 'Over thirty-three million people follow Britney Spears on Twitter? FTW!'

Fuckboy/fuck boy (noun)

Someone who tells you exactly what you want to hear solely for their own advantage. Can be recognised by the fact that they are manipulative, conniving, selfish, devious – and they want to get in your pants.

Fuck buddy (noun)

A less friendly term for *Friends with benefits*.
See also, FWB

Fucktard (noun)

A contraction of the words 'fucking' and 'retard'; someone who, regardless of their actual mental well-being, is so unbelievably and monumentally dumb that no other word will suffice.

NB, a fucktard is even more stupid than a *dumbtard*.

E.g. 'Read about that guy who tried to french kiss that Doberman? What a fucktard!'

See also, *Fuckwit*

Fuck that noise!/fuck this noise! (interjection)

A way of indicating that you do not want to comply with an instruction. A way of saying, 'I do not agree with that,' or, 'There is no possibility that I will let that happen.' A more inventive way of saying, 'Screw that!' Sometimes abbreviated to FTN.

E.g.

Manager: 'And you have to wear this chicken outfit and squawk loudly as you're handing out leaflets for the restaurant.'

You: 'Fuck that noise.'

Fuck that shit!/fuck this shit! (interjection)

An alternate way of saying *fuck that noise!* Also abbreviated to FTS.

Fuckwit (noun)

Someone who is so stupid that it defies comprehension.

E.g. 'Why do you want my phone number? You just called *me*! You're such a fuckwit!'

Fugly (adjective)

'Fucking ugly,' said without swearing. Describes someone or something that is beyond ugly; a state where even the phrase *über* ugly cannot adequately describe the amount of ugliness going on.

See also, *Baggable, Butters*

Funcrazy (adjective)

Someone who's the life and soul of any social event or something that's exceedingly enjoyable.

Fungry (noun)

A combination of 'fucking' and 'hungry', this is the emotional state that occurs before actual starvation. Being fungry usually coincides with this pronouncement, 'I need fucking food and I need it fucking now.'

See also, *Hangry*

FWB (noun)

Friend with benefits; a couple who aren't in a committed relationship but who indulge in casual no-strings sex. Every male's fantasy; all the fun and none of the emotional angst (or Valentine's Day gifts).

See also, *Fuck buddy*

Gameaholic (noun)

Someone with such a compulsion to play videogames that it's almost an addiction.

Gamble and lose (verb)

When you decide to fart but accidentally (and totally unexpectedly) shit, soiling your underwear in the process.
See also, *Shart*

Game over! (noun)

When any given situation ends in failure.
See also, *Game over, man! Game over!*

Game over, man! Game over! (verb)

When something ends in complete and utter disaster and there is absolutely no chance of redemption.
E.g. 'My mum found my copies of *Big Boob World* and *Lickety Split* under my bed and it was like, Game over, man! Game over!'

Gangsta (adjective, noun)

Not to be confused with a gangster who works within the organised crime industry, a gangsta is a watered down, MTV-friendly version commonly portrayed in rap videos. Gangstas may talk the talk and walk the walk (although baggy, wide-legged jeans pulled way down below their waist makes this difficult) but that's where the similarity ends. The baddest thing gangstas tend to do is spray graffiti on abandoned buildings, smoke weed and park in handicapped spaces.

See also, *tool*

Gasman (noun)

Someone dating an older woman, so-called because he is, in effect, servicing an old boiler.

Gazillion (noun)

A imaginary number used to signify an extremely large amount; even more than a zillion.

E.g. 'I had to go shopping with my *rents* and must've been in this furniture store for like a gazillion years!'

Geek (noun)

Geeks may take many forms, e.g. science geeks, history geeks, maths geeks, computer geeks, comic book geeks, gaming geeks etc., but what they all have in common is the following:

(a) Their interest in a non-mainstream subject.
(b) They demonstrate an excessive enthusiasm for their chosen interest to the point of psychotic obsession.
(c) They are socially awkward.
(d) They will end up earning ten times what you will.

See also, *Dork, Neek, Nerd*

Get off (verb)

To get amorous with someone. This could be anything from a lingering kiss or light groping to actual sex or any stage in between. Teen getting-off usually occurs at parties in bathrooms or the bedroom where people put their coats and traditionally is the consequence of excessive alcohol consumption. Getting off is usually followed by the following five stages: disappointment, embarrassment, regret, repercussions and recriminations.

See also, *Make out, Suck face*

GF (noun)

This means girlfriend although some people have interpreted it as grandmother or grandfather. This is wrong . . . in many senses.

GFY (interjection)

Everyone understands this as meaning 'Go fuck yourself!' except parents who for some reason, think it means 'Good for you!' and use it as an indication of approval.

E.g.
You: 'I got a B in that English exam.'
Your mum: 'GFY!'
You: 'Mum???!!! WTF?'
See also, *GTH, SMD*

Ghetto (noun)

Term used to denote the *cool* and *hip* lifestyle (clothes, actions and speech) white kids associate with black kids.

E.g.
Lucy: 'Damn, girl! I wish I was ghetto.'
Latoya: 'You want to live in a densely populated, neglected, crime-ridden, impoverished area of a city?'
Lucy: 'I'd kill for your cornrows.'
See also, *Street, Urban*

Ghost/ghosting (verb)

(a) To leave suddenly and without warning, e.g. 'This party sucks. I'm ghost, guys.'

(b) To completely cease contact with someone, e.g. 'Reese loves his iguana more than me. From now on I'm ghosting him'.
See also, *Dip/dip out*

GIMF (interjection)

Google it, motherfucker. Used when someone asks a dumb question and you don't have the patience to explain it or provide an answer. NB, if the question seems particularly stupid feel free to add the word, *dumbtard*.

E.g.
Friend: 'What does "initialism" mean?'
You: 'GIMF!'
See also, *GIYF, JFGI*

Gimongous (adjective)

Something far, far, far, far, far larger than even ginormous or humungous.

E.g. 'Man, your *moobs* are well gimongous!'

GIYF (interjection)

Google is your friend. The polite way of saying *GIMF* or *JFGI*

Glammed up (adjective)

Looking attractive; usually the result of spending an hour deciding what to wear and then two further hours on your hair and makeup.

Gnarly (adjective)

Originally a surfing and skateboarding term this now enjoys wider use as a word to mean something that's really awesome/totally extreme.

Giraffiti (noun)

Graffiti that's been painted so high up on a wall or other structure that you know it's going to stay there for a long, long time.

NB, while this term could also be used to describe graffiti painted on the side of a giraffe it is rarely used in this context.

GNOC (interjection)

Get naked on cam/get nude on cam. Instruction to or from someone you're skyping/facetiming/IMing or any form of video chatting.

NB, in some conversations GNOC might actually mean global nitrous oxide calculator, a tool to calculate soil N_2O emissions from the cultivation of potential biofuel feedstock. This is an indication that you are communicating with a science geek rather than a perv.

See also, *NIFOC*

Go double rainbow (verb)

To get *batshit* excited about something that actually doesn't justify that degree of enthusiasm or intense joy.

E.g. 'He saw my new hairstyle and went double rainbow over it. It was almost a full-blown *spaz attack!*'

Go figure! (interjection)

Something to add to the end of a sentence when you've told someone a fact and you want to emphasise that fact is surprising, unexplainable or unbelievable. An alternative to saying, *WTF!*

E.g. 'Formula songs and a total charisma void . . . yet Take That are still huge! Go figure!'

Giraffiti

Go HAM (verb)

To go as hard as a motherfucker. To do something to extreme or with maximum effort and determination.

E.g. 'It's the Scrabble championship tomorrow and I'm gonna go HAM!'

Go hard or go home (interjection)

An indication or instruction that you should go all out to do something or not bother at all.

See also, *TFFO*

Goss (noun)

A quick way of saying gossip. Useful when you need more time to, well, gossip.

See also, *Juicy goss*

Grandma (noun)

Someone female who looks and acts older than they should and whose outlook on a particular issue or life in general is deemed boring, unadventurous or out of date. Sometimes preceded by the phrase, *'Talk to the hand!'*

E.g.

Friend: 'I don't really want to watch that *Saw* box set followed by *Hostel I* and *II*. It's all a bit gory for me'.

You: 'Sorry it's not *The Best Exotic Marigold Hotel*, grandma!'

Grandpa (noun)

As *Grandma* but an insult aimed at men. *Duh!*

GTG (interjection)

Got to go. A way to end any typed conversation that you find tedious.

See also, *TTYL*

G2G (interjection)

A more hip way of saying *GTG*.

GTH (interjection)

Go to hell. Used when your anger or displeasure at someone is moderate rather than severe and doesn't quite justify a GFY
    See also, *SMD*

Gwop (noun)

Money; tends to be used within gang circles.
    E.g.
    Correct use: 'Homie! You got the goods? 'Cos I got the gwop.'
    Incorrect use: 'I hope I have the right gwop for the bus.'
    See also, *Scrilla*

Hammered (adjective)

Being more than drunk, but not as inebriated as to be *wasted*.
   See also, *Crunk*, *Faded*, *Lit*, *Sauced*, *Trashed*, *Turnt*

Hamstered (adjective)

The state between being drunk and being *hammered*.

Hang (verb)

To socialise with your friends. Usually involves discussing what to do; not agreeing on anything, getting bored and then all going home again.
   See also, *Kickin' it*

Hangin' (noun)

The act of being bored with your friends.

Hangry (noun)

When you're so hungry you're angry. This emotional state is usually the result of an absence of a parent or guardian in the house to make you dinner.
   See also, *Fungry*

Hard (adjective)

This can either mean to go wild or crazy or to try the best you possibly can.

E.g.

'Enzo went so hard at that house party, he was a legend.'

'Dude, I went so hard on that chemistry GCSE.'

NB, this term can also mean sexually aroused, a fact which can cause confusion among those unaware of your intended meaning (and concern about just how stimulating you actually found that chemistry exam).

Hardcore (adjective)

(a) Something that's extreme, intense, uncompromising or unrelenting. Can be used in context with a multitude of things including skateboarding stunts, bodybuilding, partying, gaming and *pron*.

(b) 'A hell of a lot of', e.g. 'She's doing double shifts all week and making hardcore money.'

(c) Fanatical or obsessive behaviour, e.g. 'He's into stamp collecting hardcore!'

See also, *Raw*

Hasbian (noun)

Someone who used to be a lesbian but who is now in a heterosexual relationship.

See also, *Wasbian, Yestergay*

Hashtag _____ (noun)

While adding the hashtag symbol (#) before relevant words is a convention on twitter to create a searchable link, the same practice can also be used in any typed conversation to convey humour or sarcasm. It's irrelevant whether the link is genuine or not and the term can also be used in spoken conversation for similar effect.

E.g.

'Mum asked if I want to see Mariah Carey with her #killmenow.'

'Check out Justin's blue Crocs #whataprick.'

See also, *Hashtag douchbag*

Hashtag douchebag (noun)

Someone who uses hashtags excessively in anything they type in the mistaken belief that they are being clever/ironic/humorous.

In effect, all they are doing is making themself look like a #dumbtard.

See also, *Hashtag*

Hater (noun)

Lurking on social media sites and forums, haters are those who are critical of someone's achievements or success or who just verbally attack them for stating a valid opinion. This hatred can be the result of (a) anger, (b) jealousy or, more often than not, (c) absolutely no fucking reason at all.

See also, *Haters gonna hate*

Haters gonna hate (interjection)

A riposte (usually uttered while walking away) that infers complete indifference to someone else's criticism, disapproval or insults. A more considered and polite comeback than just yelling, 'Fuck you!'

E.g.

Rude person: 'Hey, lard arse! You use Google Earth just to take a selfie!'

You: 'Haters gonna hate.'

Hawk (verb)

To stare intently at someone, usually making that person uncomfortable in the process. The two most popular reasons to hawk someone are:
(1) You find them attractive
(2) You think they're about to start trouble.
E.g.
Friend: 'All the time we were in that corner shop the owner was hawking us like a . . . a . . .'
You: 'Hawk?'
Friend: 'Yeah, that's the one.'

Headphone zombie/HZ (noun)

A headphone wearer totally cut off and unresponsive to the outside world, often with a glazed expression.
Warning: If the person also has a pale, bloodless appearance and a desire to eat your brain then you are probably observing a real zombie rather than a headphone one.

Heart (verb)

A way of expressing how you feel about something or someone that means more than 'like' but which does not imply as much affection as 'love'.
E.g. 'I heart you, Crunchy Nut cornflakes!'

Heated (adjective, verb)

Annoyed; frustrated; pissed-off. Also, to get yourself so riled that you want to pick a fight or actually start one.
E.g. 'When the café ran out of mac and cheese I was so heated I threatened the waitress with a hammer fight.'

Hench (adjective)

Someone very muscular or who at least looks strong and, by implication, someone you definitely don't want to upset.

See also, *Built, Ripped, Swole*

Here's the thing (interjection)

A good way to stop the flow of a conversation and regain the focus of everyone's attention regardless of what someone might have been saying or its importance.

E.g.

Friend: 'So my mum has run off with her personal trainer and my dad was so upset he hunted him down at the gym, stabbed him with a potato peeler and is now on the run with my little sister.'

You: 'Here's the thing, I've got a spare ticket for the Vamps. Anyone interested?'

Heteroflexible (noun)

Someone who's straight but who is open to a same-sex relationship with the right person, in the right circumstances (and by right circumstances, we're usually talking about the presence of alcohol).

E.g. 'Look. We were both hammered and you looked hot. I can't help it if I'm heteroflexible.'

HFFA (adjective)

Hot from far away; someone whose attractiveness diminishes the closer they get to you.

See also, *Ugly radius/ugly range*

Hiberdating (verb)

Someone who's hiberdating disappears from view (and stops socialising) because they're spending almost all of their time with their new boyfriend/girlfriend.

    E.g.

    You: 'Have you seen Marlon lately?'

    Friend: 'Nah. He met this girl at work and he's been hiberdating since November.'

High five (noun, verb)

The action of slapping someone's palm with your own above your heads. Used to indicate one of the following: agreement, pleasure, celebration, acknowledgment or an excess of testosterone.

    See also *Air five, Wi-five*

Himbo (noun)

Male bimbo; someone obsessed with their appearance/clothes. Blessed with a good body but lacking in the brain department. In essence, a stupid pretty boy as opposed to a pretty stupid boy.

Hip (adjective)

Something that's cooler than *cool*. Even cooler than ice cool or supercool.

    See also, *Amazeballs, Dope, Fly, Killer, Phunky*

Hippification (noun)

The process of adopting a hippy lifestyle or hippy-like qualities and values which include peace, love, respect for the environment and listening to shitty music.

Hippified (adjective)

Someone who has undergone *hippification.*
   E.g.
   You: 'There's Robbie. Look at him in those sandals and flared jeans, eating organic clothes and hugging that tree.'
   Friend: 'He's been totes hippified.'

Hipster (noun)

Someone whose life values include pretension and posturing but who shares many characteristics with old people, including chunky glasses, cardigans, hats, facial hair, fixed gear bikes and a love of cats, roll-ups and old vinyl.
   See also, *A-hole, Asshole, Douche, Douchebag, Wanker*

Hipstercrite (noun)

Someone who claims not to be a hipster and who mocks the whole hipster lifestyle – but who obviously is one. NB, almost all hipsters are hipstercrites.

Hit (verb)

To go to; usually refers to visiting the gym or shops.

Hit on, hitting on (verb)

The act of flirting or chatting up.
   See also, *Chirpsin'*

Hoasis (noun)

A concentrated area or zone of what seems like sexy/promiscuous women. NB, like its desert namesake, this also tends to be something that exists in the mind rather than reality.

E.g.

Friend: 'Wow! Look at Franki and her mates in the corner. That's what I call a hoasis!'

You: 'Dickwad.'

Homeboy (noun)

A close friend or your closest friend. If you really, really need to use this word, use *homie* instead. In fact, come to think about it, try not to even use the word homie.

Homie (noun)

Close friend, usually male; someone you grew up with and shared experiences with. NB, this word will sound *lame* unless you're actually in a street gang.

See also, *Dogg, Fam, Main, Mains, Peeps, Squad*

Hood (noun)

Neighbourhood; the area in which you live. Only to be used ironically, i.e. if where you live is an affluent suburb.

Hormotional (adjective)

Used to describe someone who overreacts to a situation.

E.g.

Friend: 'Sorry I started crying during the film but I'm hormotional. It's the time of the month.'

You: 'But you're a bloke . . . and we were watching *Expendables 3*.'

Horn dog (noun)

Someone (usually a male) who is *über horny* to the point of being addicted to sex and/or being incapable of controlling their sex drive. A horn dog is *up for it* continually.

Horny (adjective)

As the old-fashioned term 'randy'; to be sexually excited/ lecherous.

Hot (adjective)

Someone (male or female) who ticks one or more of the following boxes:
- Extremely good-looking.
- Sexy.
- Muscular.
- You want to have sexual relations with them.

See also, *Buff, Fit, Hott, Reem*

Hot mess (adjective)

A way to describe someone (usually female) who looks 'together' i.e. attractive, cool and in control but who indulges in actions that could be considered negative and reckless e.g. alcohol and drug abuse, orgies, petty crime or cage fighting.

Can also be used to describe someone who oozes glamour/ charm/desirability even though they are a complete emotional or psychological train wreck.

See also, *Train wreck*

Hott (adjective)

When you're hot, just more so.

See also, *Hot*

Hottie/hotty (noun)

Someone who's *hot* or *hott.*

HTFU (interjection)

Hurry the fuck up! Not just an indication of angry impatience, this term can also be used as term of inspiration or helpful encouragement (although it rarely is).

Huggle (noun)

Cross between a hug, a snuggle and a cuddle. A way of showing someone a huge amount of loving affection however the term is usually used in plural form as a way of indicating the end of an online conversation.

Hulk out (verb)

To get so incredibly pissed off that you lose the power of speech and all sense of reason – and go into fits of uncontrollable violent rage.

    E.g.

    Friend: 'Arrrghhhoooohhheeeeuugghhhaarrrgghhhhh!'

    You: 'So I got you diet not regular Coke! No need to hulk out, man!'

Hundo P (adjective)

An indication that you totally agree with a statement; a way of saying one hundred per cent.
NB If you're in a rush this can be abbreviated even further to 'hundo'.

    E.g.

    You: 'That girl in the corner is epic buff.'

    Friend: 'Hundo P, but you can bet your sorry ass she'll *boyfriend drop*.'

Hype beast (noun)

Someone who follows a trend or buys over-priced designer brands just for the sole reason of looking *dope*. A person in this position usually has access to *mad stacks*.

See also, *Label whore, Tag hag*

Hyper (adjective)

Having an excessive amount of energy. This might manifest itself in an inability to sleep or, more usually, the ability to act in an anti-social or just annoying manner.

See also, *Amp'd, Amp'd up, Cray*

Icing (verb)

Not the act of shooting someone (though it can mean this), but a drinking game involving chugging bottles of Smirnoff Ice.

IDC (interjection)

I don't care – the fact you can't even be bothered to type the full phrase just emphasises the disdain/apathy you feel towards someone or something.

NB, can cause huge confusion if interpreted as 'I do care'.

See also, *DGAF, IDGAF*

IDGAF (interjection)

I don't give a fuck. It's usual to demonstrate indifference towards something by ignoring it completely, however when you really, really, really feel you need to highlight your ambivalence then use this term. People who say IDGAF are proud to call it an attitude. The truth is, it's a paradox. After all, if you really don't give a fuck, why do you need to emphasise the fact that you don't?

See also, *DGAF*

I-eat-babies (adjective)

Term used to describe such an excessive amount of something that it's actually frightening.

E.g. 'Jeez. I don't know what he was doing but when he turned up he was I-eat-babies sweating!'

Icing

Igmo (noun)

Someone of lesser intelligence; short for ignorant moron; a more intelligent way to call someone dumb.

See also, *Ignoranus*

Ignoranus (noun)

A blend of ignorant and anus; used when you want to be that little bit extra-insulting when you need to call someone stupid or dumb.

See also, *Igmo*

IHAB (interjection)

I have a boyfriend – the acronym used when you want to let someone down gently without having to resort to the alternate phrase, 'Stay away, you creep.'

See also, *Boyfriend drop, IHAG*

IHAG (interjection)

I have a girlfriend – as per *IHAB* but rarely used since few teenage boys have regular girlfriends.

See also, *Girlfriend drop*

IHNFI (interjection)

I have (or had) no fucking idea; because honesty is usually the best policy.

iHog (verb)

Someone at a party who insists on talking control of the music by plugging in his/her own iPod regardless of what the host or other guests want to listen to.

E.g. 'Ricky iHogged that party with his lame party playlist . . . Barry Manilow, Peter Andre and Joe McElderry on heavy rotation!'

Ill (adjective)

Something that is so great it is actually sickening. Can also infer that someone possesses or demonstrates great ability or a very special talent.

E.g.

Skateboarding friend: 'I began with a gnarly anchor grind then pulled an ollie, a pole jam, a shifty, a rad bluntslide and a casperflip'.

You: 'Dude. You ill!'

See also, *Sick*

ILY (verb)

Short version of 'I love you' and usually written rather than spoken (although if it were said, it's pronounced 'ill-ee'). Although it's often used in the romantic sense, it can also be used between friends to mean I admire you; a compliment for an achievement.

NB To avoid embarrassment or confusion make sure the recipient understands your intended usage.

E.g.

You: 'Your art show was really awesome. ILY.'

Girl: 'ILY? Really? REALLY? OMG, OMG, OMG, OMG. IHNFI!'

You: 'Er . . . we need to talk'

I'm on it/I'm on this (interjection)

Something to say when you want to indicate that you're about to carry out a task.

E.g.

Girl: 'Look out . . . that man . . . in the shadows . . . he's got a gun!'

James Bond: 'I'm on it.' [shoots man]

Incredibad (adjective)

Something that is so very, very, very bad indeed. Can be used to describe something that is genuinely not good in any manner or degree (e.g. *'Hot Tub Time Machine 2* is so incredibad') or something that is knowingly bad (e.g. *Iron Sky* is so incredibad').

Ink (verb, noun)

Tattoo or the process of getting a tattoo.

E.g. 'Hey, granny. Excuse me taking my trousers and pants down but check out my new ink!'

Innit? (interjection)

Added to the end of a sentence, *innit?* can be used in one of two ways:

(1) To emphasise a statement that's just been made.
(2) As a way to seek reassurance/invite agreement.

It can mean any of the following:

(a) Isn't it?
(b) Isn't he/she?
(c) Aren't I?
(d) Aren't we?
(e) Aren't they?
(f) Aren't there?

E.g.

You: 'So, after school we're gonna go to Maccy D's, innit?'
Friend one: 'And Elissa and Tyler gonna join us, innit?'
Friend two: 'I'm gonna have a Crunchie McFlurry, innit?'

Internot (noun)

This can mean:

(a) Someone who says they don't actually use the internet. This is usually claimed as some sort of pathetic affectation. See *tool.*

(b) Someone who genuinely doesn't use the internet, e.g. your gran.

(c) Anywhere where's there's no internet availability, e.g. your gran's flat.

Interweb (noun)

A name for the internet used by people who think they are being humorous, ironic or sarcastic. They are none of these. They are dicks.

NB, this term is usually used by the same people who, when there is difficulty connecting online, or they receive a '404 not found' error, claim they have 'broken the internet'.

See also, *Dumbtard, Lame*

In your face! (interjection)

An exclamation of defiance, contempt or one-upmanship. Can also be used to signify victory against someone or something.

E.g. 'I only drank half the caramel latte – in your face, excessive sugar consumption.'

See also, *Boom!, Booyah!*

Irritainment (noun)

Any form of entertainment that you hate to watch but feel compelled to do so. Usually used in context with reality TV shows.

-ish (adverb)

-ish added to the end of a word means 'sort of' or 'kind of' and can be used as a reply to a question.

E.g.

You: 'Dinner at nine-ish. You hungry?'

Friend: 'Ish'

NB, when used in conjunction with a period of time it means plus or minus thirty minutes. Ish.

Jack (verb)

To steal.

 E.g.
 Friend: 'Hey. My phone's been jacked!'
 You: 'What are you calling me on, fucktard?'
 Friend: 'Oh yeah . . .'

Jealz (adjective)

See *jel/jells*

Jel/jells (adjective)

Short form of 'jealous'. Usually proceeded by *well*.
 See also, *Jelbags*

Jelbags (adjective)

The act of being slightly more envious than just being jel.
 E.g. 'Did you see the car her mum bought her. I was sooo jelbags!'
 See also, *Jel/jells*

JFGI (interjection)

Just fucking google it.
 See also, *GIMF, GIYF*

Juicy goss (noun)

Exceptionally salacious, scandalous and, hopefully, incriminating rumours about someone.

NB, these do not have to have any basis in fact.

Subjects often mentioned in juicy goss

Relationships, boob jobs, anorexia, crying, zits, fashion sense, sugar daddies, self-harm, STIs.

Subjects rarely mentioned in juicy goss

The Large Hadron Collider, pottery, the future of the Euro, Oliver Cromwell, chlorophyll.

See also, *Goss*

Junk (noun)

A catch-all term for the male genitals (component parts may also each be referred to as 'junk').

Junk in the trunk (noun)

A way to describe a woman's large, round bottom.

NB, this is traditionally used as a term of affection rather than abuse.

Kamikaze (noun)

A drink made from combining measures of all available drinks, usually at a party. This can include spirits, beer, juice and carbonated drinks. But especially spirits.

Because of the random nature of the composition, no two kamikazes are the same although the results tend to be similar; a feeling of severe nausea followed by vomiting.

Kanye (noun, verb)

This tribute to Kanye West can mean:
   (a) To rudely interrupt someone talking in order to voice an opinion absolutely no one agrees with (i.e. to act like a *douchebag*).
   (b) Someone full of their own self-importance and an inflated sense of self-worth (i.e. a *douchebag*).

Kardashian (adjective, noun)

This can mean:
   (a) Someone who's talentless, vapid, useless and shallow. Can be used for both male and females.

   E.g. 'Sure, that new guy is really fit but he's as dumb as a box of rocks. What a Kardashian!'

   (b) A period of time measuring seventy-two days (the length of Kim Kardashian's marriage to basketball star Kris

Humphries). Used to denote a short period of time rather than being used literally.

E.g. 'Only half a Kardashian 'til the end of term!'

Kewl (adjective)

An alternative (but completely unnecessary) way of writing 'cool'. A sure sign that you're a teenage girl or a *loser.*

Kickass/kick ass (verb, noun)

Yet another word for something that is cool, memorable, amazing or exceptional. Can be used to describe an inanimate object (e.g. 'That was a kickass drum kit!') or an action (e.g. 'That drummer really kicked ass!').

Kickin' (adjective)

Anything that's awesome and/or stylish.

E.g. 'Check out those kickin' kicks.'

Kickin' it (verb)

To spend time with someone or some friends, doing absolutely nothing constructive.

E.g.
Friend: 'What you doing?'
You: 'At Carlo's house. Just kickin' it.'
Friend: 'Bored?'
You: 'Hell, yeah!'
See also, *Hangin'*

Kicks (noun)

Why say 'shoes' when you can use this word that not everyone knows nor understands?

E.g. 'My new kicks are sick.'

Kill/kill it (verb)

To kill something in this sense is to receive a huge amount of praise, usually for a performance of some sort.

E.g. 'Saw you do *Green Eggs and Ham* at the poetry slam. Man, you killed it!'

See also, *Smash, Slay*

Killa/killer (adjective)

Something that is exceptional or strong/powerful. This term is just as relevant being used to describe drain cleaner as it is music.

E.g. 'That new album from the Killers is killer!'

See also *Amazeballs, Cool, Dope, Hip, Savage, Swag*

Knitting (verb)

Euphemism for any prolonged activity that takes place in the bathroom. Could refer to reading, playing *Candy Crush*, checking Facebook, defecating or masturbating (though it's normally the latter).

E.g.

You: 'What the hell are you doing? You've been in there twenty minutes with my copy of *Foamy Boobs*!'

Friend: 'Leave me alone. I'm knitting.'

Krunk (adjective)

An alternative (and more *hip* way) way of spelling *crunck*.

L

Label whore (noun)

Someone with no ability or inclination to choose the clothes that are comfortable or suit them and instead only buy designer brands (often numerous items from the same brand) to make up for their own insecurities.

See also, *Hype beast*

Lacostitute (noun)

Someone (male or female) who engages in *douchebag* activity for payment. In this case, douchebag activity involves wearing a small alligator on items of designer clothing and payment involves paying extortionately over the odds.

See also, *Abercrazy, Aberzombie, Label whore*

Lame (adjective)

Something or someone that is pathetic, unoriginal or unfunny. The complete opposite of being a *legend*.

See also, *Basic, Wack*

Lamesauce (adjective)

The complete opposite of *awesomesauce*.

Lapcorn (noun)

The popcorn that doesn't quite make the journey from carton to mouth in the cinema.

Lappy/lappie (noun)

Any laptop computer. A way of accessing pornography wherever you are.

Laters (adverb)

See you later/talk to you later. Method of ending a conversation, typed or spoken.
Sometimes followed by the words *dude* or *bro*.

Leanover (noun)

Similar to a hangover but not as extreme. Symptoms include a slight headache and fatigue but, unlike a hangover, usually accompanied by a full recollection of the events associated with the previous night's drinking.

Legend (noun)

Anyone whose reputation makes them worthy of great respect. While Nelson Mandela and Leonardo da Vinci might be worthy of this accolade, so too are that guy who played *Grand Theft Auto V* for eighteen hours straight or that girl who advertised her party on Facebook and ended up with 427 gatecrashers.

Legit (noun)

Something that is authentic, true and/or of excellent quality. Can refer to people or objects and can also be used to mean *cool*.
   E.g. 'That twelve-inch active bass sub-woofer puts out 1200 watts and that's legit!'
   See also, *Real*

Lesbro (noun)

A close straight male friend of a lesbian.
   E.g.

Friend: 'Are Cathy and Marcus a couple?'
You: 'You A-hole! She's gay! He's just her lesbro.'

Libe/libes (noun)

Shortform of the word library. Rarely used by teenagers (the slang or the facility).

Lifehack/life hack (noun)

A trick or tip designed to solve a *first world problem*.
E.g.
Friend: 'When I go out I stuff my money into a sanitary towel wrapper. No one's gonna steal that.'
You: 'Great lifehack!'

Lightweight (noun)

Someone with a laughable low alcohol tolerance or anyone who can't handle their drink.
E.g. 'Ash *ralphed* three times after necking just eight Jägerbombs. What a lightweight!'

Linner (noun)

A meal between lunch and dinner. The pm equivalent of brunch. Can also be used to describe a very late lunch.

Linkin' (verb)

Confusingly, this term can be used to describe a couple who have just started going out together as well as the next stage in the relationship when they are formerly dating each other.
E.g.
Friend: 'Me and Josie are linkin' but I hope it leads on to linkin'.'
You: 'Fo' sho'.'

Lipsin (verb)

Kissing energetically but less aggressively than in a full-on snog.

Liptease (verb)

To pout, purse, lick or bite your lips in a suggestive and teasing manner that implies you want to or are about to kiss someone. The term can also be used to describe someone putting on lipstick in a provocative manner.

Lit (noun)

(a) Something that is so, so, so cool.
See also, *Bumpin'*, *Poppin'*
(b) The state of being so drunk or stoned that all you can do is smile.
See also, *Crunk, Faded, Hammered, Sauced, Trashed, Turnt, Wasted*

LK/L-K (adjective)

Low key, as in keeping something a secret. E.g. 'Keep it LK but I think I'm pregnant and your dad's the father.'

LMAO (verb)

Laughed (or laughing) my ass off – used online only; indicates something someone finds hilarious but which, in all probability, isn't.
See also, *LMFAO, LOL, ROFL*

LMFAO (verb)

Laughed (or laughing) my fucking ass off – when you find something sooo hilarious that a mere LMAO just won't do.
See also, *LMAO, LOL, ROFL*

Lo-Fi/Low-Fi (adjective)

(a) Something ordinary or undistinguished, e.g. 'Last night was pretty lo-fi. I read, watched Netflix and cut my toe nails.'

(b) Something low-grade or unsophisticated in terms of quality, e.g. 'You've still got an iPhone 5? That's sooo low-fi.'

LOL (verb)

Laugh out loud or laughing out loud; used to indicate or emphasise something amusing in online conversations. In reality, this phrase has become so overused that it has lost its original impact and is now often gratuitously tacked on to the end of posts where it is completely irrelevant or inappropriate.

E.g. 'Can't talk. In class now. LOL,' or, 'Can't hook up later. Got aunt's funeral. LOL.'

See also, *LMAO, LMFAO, ROFL,*

Lolarious (adjective)

Something that is far, far funnier than just being mere hilarious. In reality anything described as *lolarious* is usually not funny at all.

Lolarrhoea (noun)

The result of laughing so intensely that you shit yourself.

Lolcat (noun)

Any photograph of a cat doing something innocuous with a caption superimposed on to it (usually in bad English) that the sender finds hilarious but which, at best, can be more accurately described as 'mildly amusing'. E.g. a very fat cat with the caption, 'Me is morbidly fluffy.'

Lol o'clock (noun)

7.07 am (viewed upside down on a digital alarm clock), used to represent any time that's far too early.

Loltard (noun)

Term of abuse for someone who uses *LOL* excessively and usually completely unnecessarily in all communications.

E.g.

Friend: ' . . . and then I accidentally put two sugars in my tea when I usually just take one. LOL!'

You: 'Fucking loltard.'

Longcut (noun)

This can mean:
  (a) The long way round to get somewhere; the route taken when you're in no hurry or actually want to arrive late.
  (b) A shortcut that turns out to take longer than anticipated or which actually saves no time at all.

Loser (noun)

A catch-all term for someone who doesn't confirm to the ideals of mainstream society, who *sucks* at generally everything they do and has no friends.

To signify that someone is a loser, it is customary to look at them while by making an L with your right hand and holding it to your forehead. Making this sign with your left hand doesn't make sense... you end up with a backwards 'L' and this probably singles you out to be a loser yourself.

See also, *Tool*

Lose your shit (verb)

The state of suffering a mental breakdown where you can no longer be responsible for your actions.

E.g. 'If I hear "Call Me Maybe" by Carly Rae Jepsen one more fucking time I swear I am so gonna lose my shit!'

See also, *Spaz attack, Spazzy*

Loved up (adjective)

Often used sarcastically, this means being in a relationship that is typified by *ghosting* your *mains* and being excessively and uncharacteristically romantic.

Low key (adjective)

See *LK/L-K*

LOWL (verb)

The process of laughing so much that you're actually howling; a reaction when something is far, far, far more than just *LOL* and a stage just before *LTIP* and *Lolarrhoea*.

LTIP (verb)

Laugh 'til I puked, or, Laughing 'til I puked. Pretty obvs really . . .
    See also, *Lolarrhoea*

Lurve (verb)

The word love mis-spelt by someone very annoying who wants to appear extra cutesy and who thinks it means more than just plain old love. Anyone using this term deserves some form of punishment.

Mad (adjective)

    (a) An experience that is more than exciting and even better than exhilarating, e.g. 'That bungee jump was well mad!'
    (b) Extremely, very or really, e.g. *'Halo 5* is mad cool!'
    See also, *Well*

Madd (adjective)

Alternative spelling of Mad. Used when texting/typing to emphasise just how unbelievably sensational a situation is.
E.g. 'U wanna get dreads? WTF. That's madd!'
    See also, *Mad*

Mad Stacks (noun)

The modern equivalent of 'Loadsamoney!' (Kids, ask your parents). A way of describing an excessive amount of money.
    See also, *Bank, Ends*

MAF (adjective)

Mad as fuck – when *arsed up* or *heated* don't even come close to describing just how pissed off you are.

Make groceries (verb)

A phrase to use when you want to make the act of food shopping sound vaguely interesting.

Make out (verb)

See *get off, suck face.*

Main/mains (noun)

Your closest or most important friend or friends. The collective noun for your mains is *Squad.*

  See also, *Fam, Homie, Peeps*

Man boobs (noun)

See *moobs*

Mandals (noun)

Fugly and unfashionable black or brown leather, open-toed male sandals that traditionally reveal oversize, misshapen and even more *fugly* big toes.

Manga cow (noun)

Someone who confuses the term 'comic book store' with 'library' and overstays his welcome by staying there for hours on end, grazing among the manga.

Manicorn (noun)

Mythical creature sought by females. A man who's loyal, chivalrous, funny, romantic, passionate, cultured and sensitive – and who doesn't get wasted and get off with your best friend behind your back.

Mank/manky (adjective)

Something rotten or disgusting looking, usually with a resultant smell; more foul than something that is merely grungy. Ubiquitous term that can be applied to anything from the three-week-old

Mandals

tuna sandwich you rediscover at the bottom of your backpack to a student house bathroom.

Mantrum (noun)

A male hissy-fit, usually over something very minor and inconsequential.

Maybs (adverb)

Fashionable way of expressing that something might be a possibility.

 E.g.

 You: 'Dudes! What say we all go back to mine and get *crunk?*'

 Friend one: 'Defs.'

 Friend two: 'Mos def.'

 Friend three: 'Maybs.'

 You: 'Maybs?'

 Friend three: 'I got geography homework to finish.'

McJob (noun)

A monotonous, menial soul-crushing job (usually in the service industry) with low prospects and even lower pay, usually filled by teenagers. McJobs usually involve the employee wearing a polyester uniform and working near hot oil.

 E.g.

 You: 'Nice uniform, dickwad. Three years in uni and all you could get was this McJob?

 Friend: 'McFuck you!'

Meg (noun)

Plain-looking, drab, unfashionable female who tries too hard to fit in and usually has to correct people who assume she's a boy. There are two responses when a Meg asks a question: (a) Ignore her, (b) Say, 'Shut the fuck up, Meg.'

Mega (adjective)

This term can be used in three ways:
  (1) To describe something that's *awesome,* excellent, brilliant, wonderful etc., e.g. 'That greasy kebab was mega!'
  (2) For intensification or emphasis, e.g. 'Man . . . I felt mega sick afterwards.'
  (3) To describe something that's *gimongous,* e.g. 'Don't go in the bog for at least an hour. I just dropped something mega in there.'

Meh (interjection)

A verbal shrug; an exclamation of complete indifference.
  See also, *Whatever!*

Mental hairball/Mental furball (noun)

Anything you say that's utterly random and usually completely out of context with the discussion you're having.
  E.g.
  You: 'What do you think of Liverpool's chances this week?'
  Friend: 'Camel-trousers-Bieber.'
  You: 'WTF.'
  Friend: 'Soz. Mental hairball.'
  See also, *Brainfart*

Mentalist (noun)

Someone who's eccentric, crazy, reckless or obsessive. Or all of therm.
  See also, *Cray*

Merch (noun)

Overpriced and shoddy branded T-shirts, hoodies, sweatshirts, patches, baseball caps, beanies, stickers, posters, lighters etc., etc.

offered for sale at gigs. Merch is sold on stands manned by sad people, delusional enough to really believe that they're 'with the band'.

Merk (verb)

- (a) To beat up or hurt someone.
- (b) To beat someone in a contest (anything from playing five-a-side to *Call of Duty: Black Ops III*.
- (c) To insult someone
- (d) To kill someone

Merked (adjective)

This can mean anything from being drunk or high and dishevelled to injured or killed. It can also mean failing horrendously or being the victim of verbal abuse, usually trash-talk by a rapper.

E.g. 'Man? Are you merked or what? Forgetting those lyrics? Merked! And that MC? You was well-merked! That bruv needs to be merked!'

Mike Ugly (adjective, noun)

Nickname for any male considered unattractive, regardless if his name is actually Mike or not.

E.g.

Girl one: 'Did you see that creep trying to get off with Perrie?'

Girl two: 'I know. He was so Mike Ugly.'

Girl three: 'I think he was Mike Ugly's uglier brother.'

MILF (noun)

Acronym: mother (or mum) I'd like to fuck. Basically, any one of your friend's mums you find physically attractive and sexually desirable. The perennial fantasy of teenage boys (and their fathers).

Mindfuck (noun)

Something that messes with your mind so much that it can make you question previously held beliefs and how you see the world – or just leave you very confused. Mindfuck movies include *Fight Club*, *Memento*, *Inception*, *Interstellar* and *Shutter Island*. They do not include anything starring Adam Sandler, Vinnie Jones or Jennifer Aniston.

Minger (noun)

More than just being ugly, being called a minger implies that a female is also promiscuous, common and looks like she has little or no interest in feminine hygiene. Sometimes spelt 'minga'.

Mis-wave (noun)

To wave back at someone you think is waving at you but who was actually waving to someone behind you. The mis-wave is followed immediately by a feeling of stupidity and embarrassment and a look of complete bewilderment from the stranger.

Mkay/MK (interjection)

A combination of 'ermmm' and 'okay' used when you want to agree with something but there's still a tiny lingering doubt that you might not agree fully with it.

    E.g.

    You: 'So . . . we all set to go naked moped riding?'

    Friend: '. . . Mkay.'

Mofo (noun)

Abbreviation for motherfucker. Unlike the full word, the use of 'mofo' tends to be a term of endearment or a sign of respect rather than an insult.

Mojo (noun)

Used to describe various aspects of what constitutes 'cool':
  (a) Charisma.
  (b) Sex appeal/sex drive.
  (c) Talent.
  (d) Personality.
  (e) Self-confidence.
  In males it is also the power behind a *boner.*
  E.g.
  You: 'Get off with Bianca last night?'
  Friend: 'Nah. I was tired. Lost my mojo.'

Monster! (adjective)

Another way of saying *amazeballs, awesome* or *wicked.*
  E.g.
  Friend: 'I'm going to Loch Ness.'
  You: 'Monster!'
  Friend: 'Maybs.'

Moobs (noun)

Alternative and far more evocative term for *man boobs,* flabby male breasts often found on overweight men. NB, there is only one thing more unappealing than moobs; sweaty moobs. And there's only one thing more unappealing than sweaty moobs; hairy sweaty moobs.

Moobment (noun)

The unsettling (and usually unnerving) movement of *moobs,* usually seen at a gym, on a trampoline or bouncy castle.

MOS (noun)

Mum over shoulder – an alert to a friend that what you're typing or texting has been compromised or, more often, a signal that you're bringing the conversation to a premature end because your mother is paying close attention to what you're doing.
 See also, *PAW*

Mos def (interjection)

Most definitely; what to say when you have absolutely no doubt about something.

Mouse potato (noun)

Someone who spends most of their time in front of a computer, usually playing games or surfing the net rather than doing anything that's actually constructive.
 See also, *Vidiot*

Mouthbreather/Mouth breather (noun)

Somebody who didn't bother to attend one of the evolutionary classes and missed the part about breathing through their nose. They stand around with their mouths gaping open looking exceedingly unintelligent. In effect, a very dumb person.
 See also, *Basic, Dumbtard, Fuckwit, Fucktard*

Muffin top (noun)

Roll of unsightly stomach, side and back flab that hangs over someone's waist when they wear something with a tight waistband. There is only one way that a muffin top can be considered appealing; on an actual muffin.

Munchies (noun)

One of the side-effects associated with smoking marijuana; a desperate craving for sweets and snacks, usually junk food.

Munter (noun)

Someone who fell out of the *fugly* tree and hit their face on every branch on the way down. Then had the whole tree fall on their face.
See also, *Minger/minga, Ratchet*

My bad!/my B! (interjection)

What to say when you want to say 'sorry' without actually making a genuine heartfelt apology. A short way of saying, 'Okay, so I might have made an error but you know what, I don't give a rat's arse about it so let's just get over it and move on.'
E.g.
Anne Frank: 'Dad! Don't play your drums here. Do you want the Germans to hear you?'
Anne Frank's father: 'My bad!'
See also, *Fauxpology, Oop!*

N and C (adjective)

Netflix and chill – usually used in an invitation to someone to come over and hang out, watching Netflix. It can also be used as another term for booty call. Make sure whoever you're inviting over understands your intentions.

Naff (adjective)

A lame way of saying *lame*.

Nahmean? (interjection)

Do you know what I mean? NB, this is a rhetorical question that can be added to any statement.
 See also, *Naymsayin'?*

Nahmsayin'? (interjection)

Do you know what I'm saying? Use this when you think you've been overdoing *nahmean?*

Name shame (noun)

The realisation that you are too far into a conversation with someone to ask their name on the basis that (a) you should know it already and (b) the other person assumes you know it already and would be insulted to find out you don't.

E.g. 'Talk about complete name shame! I was talking to this guy for, like, fifteen minutes when I thought to myself, You've been sitting next to me in class for almost a year and I still don't know who you are!'

Naplash (noun)

Very minor whiplash caused by starting to fall asleep somewhere where you shouldn't (usually in class), subconsciously realising what's happening, then suddenly jerking your head upright again.

Nappy (adjective)

Feeling the need to sleep.

E.g. 'Just the thought of her telling us every single mind-numbingly dull detail all about her date with Pepe is making me nappy.'

NARP (adjective)

Not a real person – used to describe someone with qualities that are so fantastically amazing that they are almost god-like.

E.g.

You: 'Did you know Jessie plays eleven different stringed musical instruments?'

Friend: 'I know! And with her teeth!'

You: 'She's so NARP!'

Nastified (verb)

Something that has become *nasty*.

Nasty (adjective)

One word; many different meanings:

(a) Disgusting.

(b) Dirty.

(c) Mean.

(d) Offensive.

(e) Spiteful.

(f) Extreme.

(g) Deviant.

Oh, yes . . . it can also mean cool or attractive.

NBD (interjection)

No big deal – usually sarcastic, to emphasise just what a big deal something is, or a way of bragging about something in a subtle way.

E.g. 'I was trying to find the loo in this club when I went the wrong way and accidentally ended up in a private party held by Jay Z and Beyoncé and they invited me to stay and I ended up snogging with Taylor Swift. NBD.'

Neat (adjective)

Something that's wonderful, awesome, cool etc.

Neat freak (noun)

Someone who's OCD about being tidy/clean/organised.

Neat beets! (interjection)

A variation on *cool beans*.

Neck (verb)

To greedily (and often quickly) drink something.

Neek (noun)

Someone who is part *nerd* and part *geek*. Many teens view this terrifying state as the equivalent of having cancer and hepatitis C simultaneously.

Neg (verb)

A backhanded compliment, usually said by a guy to get the attention of really hot girl who gets chatted up so often she is probably immune to conventional compliments. The concept of the neg is to bring the girl down to your level, taking advantage of the fact that interaction is better between equals. It also makes you stand out from the hoard of *losers* who are probably *hitting* on her all night.

NB, this technique does not work. What appears to you as a well-thought out pick-up strategy make you just sound like a rude *dork*.

E.g.

Ordinary compliment: 'Wow. I love your hair.'

Neg version: 'Wow. I love your hair. It's from a bottle, right?

Negatude (noun)

A negative attitude. More than just being pessimistic, someone with a negatude can bring down and demotivate a whole group.

Nerd (noun)

Someone who is exceedingly academic and clever but also exceedingly socially and physically awkward. Easily recognised by the following attributes: glasses, acne and being unfit (too fat or too skinny) and through the wearing of fashion that would be ironic on anyone else but in their case is just a disaster. Nerds are what your parents used to call 'drips' or 'squares'.

See also, *Dork, Dweeb, Neek, Geek*

Newb/newbie (noun)

Someone who is inexperienced or new to a particular situation. Usually refers to someone in an online gaming community but the term can also apply to someone new to a class or a job. Unlike a *noob*, *newbs* are aware of their status; don't assume they know it all and are willing to learn.

NIFOC (verb)

Naked in front of computer – whether you're on webcam or not it's important to remember that if you find the notion sexy and appealing, there are probably at least thirty times that many that find it repellent. The key to avoiding embarrassment and social exclusion is knowing your audience. If you *are* using a webcam then consider the feelings of whomever you're naked in front of. They cannot unsee this.

See also, *GNOC*

Ninety-Nine per cent (adjective)

A derogatory term for something that's either mainstream or *basic*.

E.g. 'That party started off kickass then all those kids from school turned up and it became nine-nine per cent. That's when I bailed.'

Ninja sex (noun, verb)

Discrete, silent sex required when parents/housemates are asleep. This means no groaning voices or creaking springs. Also refers to having sex undetected in a public place.

Nodel (noun)

Someone who really thinks they're a model (e.g. they might have appeared in a low budget advertising campaign for hair extensions), but who clearly isn't.

NIFOC

No flex zone (noun)

Anywhere you can chill out with friends without the risk of someone boasting about their achievements and/or material goods.

See also, *Flexin'*

Nom, nom, nom (interjection)

See *om nom nom*

Noms (noun)

Food.

E.g. 'Gimme noms. I'm fungry!'

Nonversation (noun)

A conversation that's pointless and usually awkward, e.g. you don't learn anything from it, it's probably boring and you can't wait for it to end. Often occurs when you bump into someone you haven't seen for at least five years and/or you've been desperately trying to avoid.

See also, *Talkward*

Noob (noun)

Originally used to describe someone who's new to a particular videogame, the term can now be used to describe someone inexperienced in anything. What noobs have in common is that they are absolutely useless, lacking any degree of skill or competence, think they know it all but are not willing to learn or be taught. In summary, whatever they are doing, they suck.

The term can also be used as an insult for someone who's experienced but who makes a dumb rookie mistake.

See also *Newb/newbie*

Noogie (noun)

The act of energetically rubbing your knuckles or fist into someone's head to cause annoyance, pain and hair displacement. It's a male thing.

No problemo (interjection)

Used when you want to say, 'No problem', but you find you have a little more time on your hands.

Nugs (noun)

This can refer to either a small chunk of cannabis or chicken nuggets. While the wrong interpretation can be amusing in some circumstances it's worth remembering that most drug pushers are not known for their sense of humour.

Nuts, the (adjective)

Something of unsurpassed quality; the absolute best of its kind. Usually used by males as an alternative for *awesome*.

Obeast (adjective)

Someone who combines a planet-sized degree of ugliness and is so massively overweight that they look like they have their own gravitational pull.

Obvi/obvee (adverb)

See *obvs*

Obvs (adverb)

Pronounced with a silent 'b' this is the quick way to say 'obviously' and is a convenient way to end a sentence without having to say or type something like, 'Of course I know that, you twat.'
    E.g.
    Physics teacher: 'The Planck-Einstein relation connects the particulate photon energy with its associated wave frequency.'
    You: 'Obvs.'

OH (verb)

Not an exclamation of mild surprise but an acronym for 'overheard'. Usually followed in a conversation by some form of *goss* or *juicy goss*.

Old school/old skool (noun)

Anything that took place before the year 2000.

OMFG! (interjection)

Oh my fucking god! The far more dramatic version of *OMG!*, used when something is astounding rather than surprising, or repugnant rather than disgusting.

See also, *OMG!*

OMG! (interjection)

Similar to *WTF!*, this acronym for 'Oh, my god!' is used to express feelings of surprise but also disgust. Parents and religious people tend to disapprove of the meaning on the grounds that it's taking the name of the Lord in vain; instead, their preferred interpretation is, 'Oh, my gosh' (or, for the very religious or easily offended, 'Oh, my goldfish!').

NB, OMG! tends to be used in written communication; those who speak the initials out loud tend to be teenage girls.

See also, *OMFG!*

Omniblow (noun, verb)

(a) Someone or something that fails at every single thing they do; they are the epitome of universal shittiness.
(b) Something that blows *absofuckinglutely*.

See also, *Blow*

Omnishambles (noun)

Something or someone that, whatever way you look at it, is a complete fuck-up.

Om, nom, nom (interjection)

Originally the noise made by Cookie Monster from *Sesame Street* whenever frenziedly consuming the food that gave him his name, this sound or phrase has been adopted to indicate that something is particularly appetising. Can be used before, during or after consumption.

   E.g.

   You: 'I could murder a big greasy kebab right now, or maybe a bucket of wings.'

   Friend: 'Om, nom, nom.'

On and poppin' (adjective)

The state of being *cool, on trend* and *funcrazy*. This is usually used to describe things like a party, a holiday or a night out, rather than a holy communion or a driving lesson.

On fire (verb)

Someone who is doing (or has done) exceptionally well at a given action, usually some sort of performance. A phrase often heard on reality TV talent shows.

   E.g. 'Man, I loved your version of 'Crazy Frog'. You totally owned it. You were on fire!'

On fleek (adjective)

Used to describe something that's perfectly styled or executed . . . usually an object of incredible significance or importance like hair, make-up, nails or eyebrows.

   E.g. 'Man, did you see Harry Style's hair? It was totally on fleek.'
See also, *On point*

Onions (noun)

   (a) Feelings for something or someone that are so intense that you really want to cry.

   (b) A highly emotional state.

On point (adjective)

(a) Something that is absolutely perfect/flawless.

(b) To be fantastically stylish.

(c) To be in absolute control of a situation.

E.g.

Friend: 'Your hair is so on point! You look on point, girl, but ain't you worried about the damn rain?'

You: 'Nah. Got a hat. I'm on point.'

See also, *on fleek*

On trend (adjectve)

Something that is popular or fashionable at that moment (but likely to be passé weeks, if not days, later). This phrase can apply to fashion, music, movies, politics, popular culture in general and also many of the words in this book.

See also, *Bang on trend, Cool, Hip, Trending*

OOMF (noun)

One of my followers – used in reference to Twitter, not your position as a cult leader. It can also mean 'one of my friends'.

Oop! (interjection)

The *on-trend* way of expressing dismay or surprise at an act of clumsiness, a social blunder or something you've said or done that is inappropriate. A way of indicating that you're sorry without actually saying sorry.

See also, *My bad!*

Out there (adjective)

Something or someone very quirky, unconventional, weird, individual or just mentally deranged.

E.g. 'His DJ set blended bang on-trend drum'n'bass with remixed sounds of toilets flushing. It was so out there!'

Outters (noun)

Out of order. This should be used in the context of something that constitutes unacceptable behaviour and not in reference to toilets, vending machines or lifts.

E.g. 'I only got a B minus for my essay on environmental determinism. That's so outters!'

Overshare (interjection)

To give more information than wanted or, indeed, necessary.

E.g.

Your mother: 'You wouldn't think so by looking at him, but your father is so tender and gentle when he makes love to me.'

You: 'Mum! Overshare!'

See also, *TMI*

Own (verb)

To own something is to exert your personal touch or personality on it and make it yours.

E.g. 'Man. You were *sick* at that karaoke. You totally owned "Wrecking Ball"!'

To own a person, see *Owned*.

Owned (verb)

To be *owned* is to be put in your place and made to look foolish either by being proved wrong, being caught out or being comprehensively beaten in a competition (usually a videogame). The person who is owned is usually embarrassed, humiliated or disgraced. Well, at least temporarily.

E.g. 'He saw that text and knew you was two-timing him. You are so owned!'

See also, *Pwned*

Par/parred (adjective, verb)

To offend someone either by insulting them, rejecting them or
ignoring them.

    E.g.

    Friend: 'That girl turned me down. Says it would be weird 'cos I
remind her of her brother.'

    You: 'She doesn't have a brother. You got parred!'

    See also, *Diss*

Party foul (noun)

An action that's deemed socially unacceptable at a party and
which is likely to compromise its success. A party foul can range
from a simple accident like spilling red wine over a new carpet, an
ill-judged prank like setting fire to the curtains or drunkenly taking
a dump in the sink.

PAW (noun)

Parents are watching.

    See also, *MOS*

PDA (noun)

Public display of affection – e.g. holding hands, kissing, hugging.
Licking and groping are not deemed affectionate so do not
constitute an act of affection. NB, the placing of hands into each

other's opposite back pockets is deemed a Pathetic Display of Affection.

Peas (noun)

A term for money, although people might think you're talking about the small round green vegetable.

E.g. 'After pulling a double shift at the veggie restaurant I've got a shit load of peas.'

See also, *Ends*

Pedostache (noun)

A thin layer of fuzz on the top lip often mistaken for dirt or grease; not even a *wannabe* moustache. A look often associated with paedophiles.

See also, *Pornstache*

Peace out (interjection)

A way of saying goodbye or see you later. If said in public the greeting can be preceded by beating your chest twice with your fist, then giving the peace sign.

Peegasm (noun)

Intense euphoric feeling experienced by men when they finally go to the bathroom (or more usually, an alley at the back of a club) after hours of procrastinated urination.

Peeps (noun)

Short for 'people' but used to describe your close friends or family rather than a large group or the overall population.

See also, *Fam, Main/mains, Squad*

Peng (noun

Not, as some believe a slang term for small aquatic flightless birds of the southern hemisphere, e.g. 'Man. Look at the flippers on that peng!', but a term that means an attractive or sexy woman.

See also, *Fit, Hot, Reem*

Percussive maintenance (noun)

Getting a mechanical or electronic device to function by striking it violently. Sometimes referred to as 'beating the living crap' out of something. NB, excess percussive maintenance can result in the device becoming permanently non-functional.

Perf (adjective)

Something that is *amazeballs* and unlikely to be improved upon.

Pfun (adjective, noun)

More than mere fun. This is pure fun.

Phat (noun)

Although still used to imply something that is cool, awesome or sexy, this word is dated and those who use it are considered to be committing a slang faux pas. The correct response to anyone using 'phat' is, 'You're a dick.'

Phoner (noun)

A phony boner; a bulge in the front pocket of tight trousers that is usually mistaken for an erection.

E.g.

Friend: 'Ew, dude. Are you that pleased to see me?'

You [looking down at front of trousers]: 'Ew, no, dude! It's just a phoner!'

Photo-bombing (verb)

The act of deliberately ruining a stranger's photo by appearing in the frame without their knowledge, making the most stupid face you can think of.

See also, *Selfie-bombing*

Phunky (adjective)

The word 'funky' has had a makeover! It still means cool/hip etc., but now you can use it without looking like some lame 1970s throwback.

Pic (noun)

Any digital photograph or image on the internet. Plural is 'pix'. Usually preceded by the words 'nude' or 'naked'.

Pie hole/piehole (noun)

The place where pies enter your face. i.e. the mouth. Usually preceded by the words, 'Shut your fucking . . .'

Piff (adjective)

Something that is better than average; usually used to describe someone's appearance.

E.g.

You: 'Man. Have you seen Yasmin? She's lookin' damn piff.'

Friend: 'Piff? More like Peng!'

You: 'Whatevs.'

Pimp (verb)

To greatly modify or improve something, in the process customising it to suit your requirements.

E.g. 'Pineapple, cajun shrimp, beer-battered calamari, fried eggs, peas *and* baked sushi? Man, you so pimped that pizza!'

Piss-easy (adjective)

An action that is exceedingly simple. The term reflects just how easy it is to urinate (well unless you suffer from a bladder infection or have prostate trouble).

Pit stick (noun)

Underarm antiperspirant/deodorant.

Plastic (adjective, noun)

Someone who's superficial and shallow; often obsessed with their appearance and social status.
    See also, *Kardashian*

Player/playa (noun)

Surprisingly not an accolade given to an Xbox addict, but instead the term given to someone who 'plays the field', i.e. a ladies man with a reputation for dating two or more girls simultaneously. Players are envied by other men and act this way because they have a deep-rooted fear of commitment. Actually that's a lie. They just like manipulating women and sleeping around.
    The variation 'playa' is often used by people trying to appear *urban*.
    See also, *Douche*

Played (verb)

To be played is to be manipulated, misled or taken advantage of in some way. There are many ways to be played but the end result is always the same; you looking like a *tool*.

E.g.

Friend: 'So Zooey broke up with me sayin' her granny had fallen off a hoverboard and she had to take care of her and wasn't ready for a relationship. Next thing I know she's dating Matt!'

You: 'Man. You were so played!'

Plex (verb)

To get in a physical or verbal fight with someone.
  See also, *Beef*

Plutoed (verb)

To be excluded from a social group that you were once very much part of. Term refers to Pluto; once considered a planet but then kicked out of the solar system as it didn't meet the updated criteria for a planet.

Pop a stiffy (verb)

To have an erection.
  See also, *Boner*

Poppin' (adjective)

  See also, *bumpin'*

Poppin' tags (verb)

The removal of price tags or security tags. This phrase can mean either shopping or shoplifting. Be careful when using this phrase since a misunderstanding can lead to, at best, confusion or, at worst, a court appearance.

Poppin' tags

Pornfolio (noun)

The secret collection of porn images stored in a folder hidden somewhere on your computer (preferably not on the desktop).

Pornstache (noun)

Moustache that looks like it belongs in a bad 1970s porn film and which makes the wearer look like a *sleazeball*.
See also, *Pedostache*

POS (noun)

Piece of shit – usually a reference to something of such poor quality that it lets you down. However, the term is often also used by teens to describe any laptop or smartphone over eighteen months old.
See also, *Posmobile*

Poser (noun)

Someone who pretends to be someone they're not (usually by the way they dress or the references they use) so they can fit in with a particular social group.
E.g.
Friend: 'So he said, "Dude, I was pumping mongo and ollied that twelve-set" but I know he doesn't even have a skateboard!'
You: 'Fucking poser.'
See also, *Fake, Wannabe*

Positutely (adverb, interjection)

When you're so, so sure about something that you're more that just being positively, absolutely, completely, definitely certain.
E.g.

Blake: 'Are you sure that from tomorrow it's okay to wear crop tops and leather micro-skirts to school?'

Lexie [sniggering]: 'Positutely!'

Posmobile (noun)

A car that's old, unfashionable or liable to break down. Often used to describe *chaviots*.

See also, *POS*

Prec (verb)

Pronounced 'preesh', this word is a quick way of showing your appreciation or gratitude.

E.g.

Friend: 'Dude. I got you a ticket to see a sing-along showing of *Frozen*.'

You: 'Prec!'

Preggers (adjective)

Pregnant. The use of this term usually (but not always) indicates a certain lack of respect, inferring that the pregnancy was unplanned.

E.g.

Friend: 'I hear Jade's preggers.'

You: 'I just thought she was just obeast.'

See also, *Preggo/prego, Pregs*

Preggo/prego (adjective)

See *preggers*

Pregret (noun, verb)

To worry about things that haven't actually happened yet, but that you know will cause disappointment or anxiety.

E.g. 'I know Stacey's wedding is a year away but I'm already having pregrets that I agreed to be a bridesmaid. I mean who wants to wear a floral peasant blouse with leopard-skin tracky bottoms, FFS?'

Pregs (adjective)

See *preggers*

Pres (noun)

Rhyming with the word 'breeze', this is the short form of the phrase 'pre-drinks' – a sort of mini-party at someone's house before the night or event actually starts. The motivation for pre-drinks isn't to become drunk quicker but that it's cheaper drinking rancid supermarket own-brand alcohol in someone's bedroom than the pricey good stuff at a bar or restaurant.

Presh (adjective)

Shortform of precious, i.e. adorable or really cute.
   E.g.
   Friend: 'Dude. I got you this two-week-old kitten called Fluffy Boo Boo.'
   You: 'Presh!'

Prime (noun and adjective)

Something that is of incomparable quality. Used to describe objects rather than people.
   Warning: A prime number is not a number that is absolutely incredible. It is a whole number larger than one that is only divisible by one and itself.
   See also, *Beast, Boss, Epic*

Primper (noun)

Someone who takes an unreasonable amount of time to get ready, making sure that every single aspect of their appearance is *on fleek*.

Probs (adverb)

Short for either probably or problems.

E.g.

You: 'Bruv. With your complete lack of qualifications and Man U tat on your face do you think you'll have probs getting into Balliol College, Oxford?'

Friend: 'Probs.'

Procrapstinate (verb)

(1) To avoid going to the toilet, e.g. when you're in the cinema, a games arcade or the exam hall.

(2) To put off doing something by taking a long dump.

Pron (noun)

The word 'porn' deliberately mis-spelled in the misbelief that someone (and by someone I mean a parent) reading an email or text over your shoulder won't realise what the word is really referring to. As perplexing to them as you typing 'RU16?' Duh!

Props (noun)

To give props to someone is to show proper respect, recognition or admiration for their actions.

E.g.

You: 'So Joey lit his fart and the flame must've been two feet long!'

Friend: 'Props!'

Proper (adjective)

(a) Something done really well, e.g. 'That was a proper punch-up.'

(b) Very, really, incredibly etc., e.g. 'I'm proper *hangry*!'

(c) Excellent, awesome etc., e.g. 'Your new apricot beret is proper!'

Psyched (adjective)

To be totally *pumped* in anticipation.

See also, *Amp'd/amp'd up/amped, Pumped, Stoked*

PTFO (verb)

Passed the fuck out – usually in the context of the aftermath of a party.

Pud (noun)

An extraordinarily weak, inept, useless and wimpy male who has no earthly chance of being anything but *lame* in absolutely everything they do. Another way of saying *pussy.*

Pull (verb)

The act of successfully attracting someone with the ultimate aim of snogging or boning them. Usually occurs at bars, parties or clubs as a result of excessive alcohol consumption by either person.

Pull a Britney (verb)

Coined in tribute to Britney Spear's 2006–7 meltdown, this means to have or to show signs of, a mental breakdown, usually as the result of excessive drugs or alcohol. Indications include, but are not limited to, shaving your hair off, driving with your child in your lap and not wearing underwear and flashing everyone when you exit your car.

Pumped (verb)

To be enthusiastically thrilled about something. More likely to be used in context with kicking someone's ass or a charity parachute jump rather than a visit to your aunty.

See also, *Amp'd/amp'd up/amped, Psyched, Stoked*

Pump it (verb)

Two opposite meanings . . . and a fight waiting to happen:
   (1) To immediately stop what you're doing, e.g. 'Bro! I know you love Aqua's "Barbie Girl" but you need to pump it!'
   (2) To make something louder, e.g. 'Bro! I know you love Aqua's "Barbie Girl" but you need to pump it!'

Punk (verb)

To fool or trick someone, usually as a result of an elaborate practical joke or prank.

Someone who falls victim to this sort of hoax is said to have been 'punk'd'.

Pussy (adjective, noun)

A mocking term used to describe a cowardly and emotionally or physically weak man. The *old skool* term for *wimp*.

See also, *Pud, Pussy-whipped*

Pussy-whipped (adjective)

Someone who's emotionally and socially dominated by his female partner. Signs of being pussy-whipped including being told where to go, what to wear, what to say and when to be home by.

Pwned (verb)

Pronounced to rhyme with 'moaned', what started as poor typing has been adopted and accepted as an alternative way to write or say 'owned'. People using this version think they are *street*. They are in fact, idiots.

See also, *Owned*

QLC (noun)

Quarter-life crisis – a period of stress and immense self-doubt that occurs in your mid-twenties when you realise you won't ever be the next Steve Jobs, Lionel Messi or Drake, and that your position as senior bought ledger clerk at a chain of garden centres is the best you can ever hope for.

Quad-boobs (noun)

The effect of a too-tight bra that causes the wearer's bosoms to spill over the top so it looks like she has four breasts.

Qwasted (adjective)

Pronounced 'kway-sted', this is a state slightly more intoxicated/ high than *wasted*.

Qwerting (verb)

The action of typing random keyboard characters in an email, text or online message to indicate frustration or disbelief.
  E.g.
  'Michael Bublé? Why would she think I want to see Michael-fucking-Bublé dlfiw898w9er89asjhu232jkjflkw!'

Qwertist (noun)

Derogatory term for someone who spends far too much time on a computer or playing with a smartphone, usually because they have very little else going on in their life.

Qwerty flirty (adjective)

To be very flirtatious through the use of *emojis*, especially the heart, lips and the face winking with its tongue out.

Quiche (adjective)

Something or someone that is hotter than hot; but as a measurement of attractiveness, not temperature.

E.g. 'This quiche is so quiche.'

Rackne (noun)

Acne found on a woman's breasts.
  See also, *Assne, Bacne, Backne, Chestne*

Rad (adjective)

Old skool term for cool, awesome etc., but back in fashion again as retro-slang.

Radar butt (noun)

The name given to your bottom when it displays the uncanny ability to sense that you're nearing home and decides that now, rather than when you actually arrive back, is the time that you absolutely, positively have to take a dump. NB, 'nearing home' can still mean thirty minutes away.

Radar sphincter (noun)

See *radar butt*

Radascular (adjective)

Something that's spectacularly *rad*.

Radastic (adjective)

Something that's fantastically *rad*.

Ralph (verb)

See *barf, upchuck*

Rando (noun)

A random person who often appears at parties but who no one seems to know, let alone to have invited. Tends to hang around the periphery of groups of friends, observing but not taking part in conversations. Randos are mainly male and usually awkward and/or creepy.

E.g.

You: 'Who was that guy listening to what you were saying to Kaylee?'

Friend: 'Just some rando. He was so *sketchy!*'

Ratchet (adjective, noun)

A corruption of the word wretched; being called or described a ratchet implies you're an out-of-control, fucked-up mess. Can be used to describe someone who's one or more of the following: obnoxious, trashy, overweight, ugly or stupid. It can also be used to refer to someone who is acting like a diva.

See also, *Hot mess, Minger/minga, Skank, THOT*

Raw (adjective)

Usually used to describe something original, pure, real, serious or intense. Can also be used to describe something that's *awesome* or *cool*, or sex without a condom.

See also, *Hardcore*

Real (adverb, noun)

This can mean all of the following:

(a) Something that's authentic or original, the 'real deal'.

Ralph

(b) The action of being true to yourself in terms of your ethics and morals, e.g. 'Keep it real, bro.'

(c) Something or someone that has no pretensions, e.g. 'Man, that drum'n'bass vibe is raw'n'real!'

(d) Having an *IDGAF* attitude, e.g. 'Stealing that Snickers bar to show support for those cocoa farmers? That's so real!'

See also, *Legit*

Reboot (verb)

Not the action of putting your shoes back on but the process of starting something afresh. Can refer to many things, e.g. a relationship, watching a box set, a diet. Can also mean the process of re-energising yourself.

E.g. 'I decided to reboot *Games of Thrones* to see if I could get into it. To get me through the first season in one night took eight cans of Red Bull and a latte.'

Redoncolous/redonkulous (adjective)

Term to describe something that's more than ridiculous; in effect the most ludicrous and preposterous thing you've ever heard or seen. Can be used in a positive way though to describe something *über-cool* or *awesome*.

See also, *Ridic, Ridoncolous/ridonkulous*

Reem (adjective)

An all-purpose term for something that is great/brilliant/fantastic. Usually used to describe someone with an attractive personality or physical appearance, it can also refer to a memorable experience or an awesome inanimate object.

See also, *Buff, Cool, Dope, Fit, Peng, Swole*

Regret ceiling (noun)

The apparent maximum amount of regret you can feel during the day. When you reach the regret ceiling you stop feeling remorseful for anything you've thought, said or done.

E.g. 'By lunchtime I'd hit my regret ceiling. If Benji's still upset that I called his girlfriend an ugmo then . . . Meh.'

Rekt (verb)

Text speak for when you got so drunk or wasted that you can't spell wrecked (although this presupposes that in this state you will be able to remember what the short form of wrecked actually is).

Relationshit (noun)

Any relationship that, for whatever reason, has gone appallingly wrong or has disintegrated to the point of non-existence. Reasons include cheating, lack of trust, lack of communication, getting clingy, substance abuse or possession by an evil spirit.

Rents (noun)

Abbreviated form of parents.

See also, *Rentsy*

Rentsy (adjective)

Acting like parents, i.e. acting responsibly or demonstrating a taste in music that's almost too nauseating to contemplate.

E.g.
Friend: 'Are you gonna be warm enough in that hoody?'
You: 'Stop being so fucking rentsy.'

Rep (noun)

A reputation (good or bad).

E.g. 'Skipping to school? Not good for my rep, bro.'

Rep your team (verb)

To represent or show support for your chosen sporting team, usually by wearing replica sportswear. However, wearing something that could be deemed 'uncool' can result in you getting a bad *rep*, e.g. there is absolutely no instance in this universe in which a replica Ipswich Town football shirt is preferable to a replica Lakers jersey.

Re-uninvite (verb)

The act of inviting someone (usually to a party), then changing your mind and saying you don't actually want them there, then changing it again because you do want their company before finally deciding that you made a mistake and you don't. NB, following such a sequence of events means this person is unlikely to ever talk to you again.

Revirginised (verb)

The effect of going without sex for so long that it begins to feel that you've regained your virginity.

Ride (noun)

Usually refers to a car but can be any type of vehicle.
   E.g.
   Friend: 'Hey, bruvs. Check out my cool new ride!'
   You: 'That's a bicycle'
   Friend: 'Yeah. But I ride it, don't I?'
   You: 'Dickwad.'

Ridic (adjective)

When you want to say 'ridiculous' in half the number of syllables.
   See also, *Redoncolous, Redonkulous*

Ridoncolous/ridonkulous (adjective)

See, *redoncolous/redonkulous*

Rinse (verb)

This can mean:
    (1) To use something up quickly, e.g. 'I was so thirsty I rinsed my Diet Fanta in one go.'
    (2) Something that's done to excess, e.g. 'Why have I put on twelve pounds? You know that whole book of Pizza Express discount vouchers? Rinsed it!'

Ripped (adjective)

Someone with well-defined muscles. They may be strong or they may not be – but you don't really want to find out.
    See also, *Built, Hench, Swole*

Rip the piss out of/rip the shit out of (verb)

To make fun of someone; to humiliate them, usually in public. This usually occurs during *bantz* or *top bantz*.

RMFE (interjection)

Roll (or rolling) my fucking eyes – used to indicate disgust or disbelief.

Road bone (noun)

An unwanted erection that can occur from the rhythmic vibration during a car, coach, train or plane journey.
    See also, *Boner*

Roast (noun, verb)

To verbally humiliate or ridicule someone in a humorous way based on their appearance, personality or actions.

E.g.

You (to friend): What the hell are you talking about? I could eat a bowl of alphabet soup and shit out a smarter statement than that!'

Other friends: 'Roast!'

Rock (verb)

To do something to great effect/impressively.

E.g. 'Lady Gaga really rocked that meat dress.'

Rocks (verb)

If something *rocks,* it is *awesome.*

Rock up (verb)

To arrive unannounced and without any forward planning; usually (but not exclusively) with your *crew.*

See also, *Roll up*

ROFL (verb)

Rolling on floor laughing. What used to be known as 'wetting your pants'.

See also, *LMAO, LMFAO, LOL*

Roll up (verb)

See *rock up.*

Roomie/roomy (noun)

The untidiest and most unhygienic person in the whole world who also wears your clothes without your knowledge.

Running latte (adjective)

Running late for a class or meeting for a good reason; you've stopped to pick up coffees on the way.

Safety chicken (noun)

The precautionary extra wings you buy from KFC or Nandos because of your uncertainty over your hunger levels.

Saggin' (verb)

A way of wearing trousers so low that your thighs or knees become in effect, your waist.

Said no one ever (verb)

A sarcastic or mocking phrase tacked on to the end of a statement that negates that same statement. The current version of 'Not!'
    E.g. 'OMG! Lovin' that brown corduroy shirt. Makes you look so fucking dope. Said no one ever.'

Sangry (adjective)

The mixed emotion of being both sad and angry at the same time. Often occurs when your team fails to qualify for the Champions League.

Sass (noun)

Someone with sass demonstrates an attitude that can range from mild cheekiness to complete and utter contempt. This trait can be attractive in a *bad boy* sort of way.
    See also, *Sasshole, Sassy*

Sasshole (noun)

Someone who tries being sassy but who lacks the charm. What's intended as humorous sarcasm just comes out as offensive.
    See also, *Sass, Sassy*

Sassy (adjective)

The state of having a large amount of *sass,* e.g. being cheeky, mouthy, cocky, sarcastic, impudent and rude – but in a quite endearing way.
    See also, *Sass, Sasshole*

Sauced (adjective)

To be very drunk.
    See also, *DAF, Faded, Lit, Hammered, Trashed, Turnt, Wasted*

Sausage fest/sausagefest (noun)

Any event (but usually a party) where the crowd is at least 80 per cent male. A sausage fest severely diminishes your opportunity for pulling.
    See, *Pull*

Savage (adjective, noun)

Used to describe an action that exceeds all expectations or someone who can be considered a *BAMF.*
    E.g. 'Two bottles of Lidl own-brand vodka and you still managed to tattoo that pic of Miley Cyrus on your chest! Dude, that was savage.'
    See also, *Amazeballs, Cool, Dope, Killer, Swag*

Say whaaat? (interjection)

What to utter after hearing surprising news. Quick way of saying, 'I find that statement hard to believe. Would you mind repeating it?'

Scando/scandy (adjective)

Scandalous, but when you want to sound more *street* or *urban*.

Schedge (noun, verb)

The short form of schedule; spoken not written and pronounced 'skedge'.

E.g. 'Dude, not sure if I can make the chess club Tuesday. Need to check my schedge.'

Scooby (noun)

An idea or a clue, used in the sense of being aware of a relevant fact.

E.g.

Friend: 'What time does the ballet start?'

You: 'I haven't got a fucking Scooby.'

Scoop (verb)

To pick someone up, usually by car.

Scoozi/scoozy (interjection, noun)

Term used to excuse yourself in either of these situations:

(a) When you pass through a crowd.

(b) When you pass wind.

The term can also be used to described an act that was committed in error and which you had absolutely no intention of carrying out.

E.g.

You: 'Man. I didn't mean to set your dad on fire like that. It was a scoozi.'

Friend: 'OK. We cool.'

Screamy (adjective)

Anything that generates loud, usually annoyingly high-pitched screams. Usually used in context with babies and toddlers – or girls watching the *Final Destination* franchise.

Seatjack (verb)

To steal someone's seat when it's left unoccupied for even a moment.

Scrilla (noun)

Money, usually bank notes; used within gang circles.
  See also, *Gwop*

Selfie (noun)

The result of taking at least six self-portraits on a phone or tablet then carefully judging the result, choosing the best shot and adjusting the brightness, colour and crop, applying filters and then uploading it to social media because you're desperate for attention.

Selfie-bombing (verb)

The act of deliberately ruining someone's selfie by appearing right behind them with a stupid expression exactly as they press the button to take the photo.
  See also, *Photo-bombing*

Selfie claw (noun)

The strange, deformed, claw-like position your hand needs to contort itself into in order to simultaneously hold your phone and take the photo.

Selfiegenic (adjective)

Someone who looks average or even *ugmo* in real life but who, for some annoying reason, always manages to look *hot* or *fit* in *selfies*.

Selfiholic (noun)

Someone addicted to taking *selfies*. Usually suffers from low self-esteem and craves attention, validation – and people saying how hot they look.

Senti (adjective)

Short form of sentimental, but usually used sarcastically to mock someone's feelings.

 E.g. 'So your mum threw out Mister Coochy your old teddy. Stop getting so senti. You're thirty-two, FFS!'

Ser (adjective, noun)

The quick way to say serious or seriously in conversation, although its use can undermine the gravity of a situation.

 E.g.

 Doctor: 'I'm afraid to say you've got cancer of the brain and it's pretty ser.'

Sexify (verb)

The act of making something or someone sexy.

 E.g. 'I think adding the pink under-car neons to my Corsa really sexify it.'

Sexiled (verb)

When you find yourself kicked out from a shared room so your roommate can have 'quality time' with his or her partner or someone they've just pulled. And by 'quality time', we're talking sex. But you knew that...

Sexiled

Sext (noun, verb)

A suggestive message with or without provocative photos sent via text or instant messaging. It is easy to tell if a text is a sext as they traditionally follow this format: 'Hey. I want to lick your [body part] then put my [body part] in your [body part] while I [sexual act].'

Sexting (verb)

The act of sending a sext.

Shady (adjective)

Someone you don't really trust or a business with questionable ethics.

See also, *Sketchy*

Shantz (noun)

Mash-up between 'shit' and *bantz*; used to describe the trading of decidedly unfunny mocking remarks.

See also, *Bantz* and *Top Bantz*

Shart (verb)

Accidentally shitting when you fart. It can be explained by the chemical reaction of gas followed by mass.

See also, *Gamble and lose*

Shiny (adjective)

Cool, neat, awesome or good in any way. Can refer to people or things.

E.g.

You: 'That Honda Civic Type R is well shiny.'

Friend: 'I know. I can see my face in the bonnet.'

You: 'No. I mean it's shiny.'

Friend: 'Yeah. Look at the sun glinting off it.'

You: 'No. It's *shiny*!'
Friend: 'I know! He must have waxed it like five times.'
You: ''tard.'

Ship (verb)

Why use four syllables to describe a romantic association when one will do just as well? The quick way to describe a couple you can so see having a relationship.

E.g. Mercutio [to Romeo]: 'You and Juliet? OMG! I can totes ship you two!'

Shitfaced (adjective)

See *DAF, faded, lit, hammered, sauced, trashed, turnt, wasted.*

Shizzle (adverb)

Out-dated slang mainly used ironically, meaning 'sure', as in, 'Of course I am certain.' It is usually preceded by the word 'fo.''

See also, *Sho*

Sho (adverb)

An expression to convey certainty; sometimes proceeded by the word 'fo''.

E.g.
Friend: 'So we can get *scooped* by Tara?'
You: 'Sho.'
Friend: 'Sho?'
You: 'Fo' sho.'
See also, *Shizzle*

Shout-out (noun)

A public acknowledgement of a friend or family member. Can be spoken, requested via an MC at an event or via a radio

DJ. Traditionally these are statements of gratitude or positive comments (i.e. you don't call someone a *douchebag* in a shout-out).

E.g.

'And for helping me with my geography revision I want to give a big shout-out to my BFF Amanda.'

Shrubble (noun)

More than stubble but not quite a beard; untidy facial hair that looks more like a small plant has taken root around your cheeks and chin.

Sick (adjective)

This can be used in two completely opposite ways:

(a) To indicate that something is extremely good or satisfying.

E.g. 'The way you just asked her out, that was sick!'

(b) To indicate that something is extremely wrong.

E.g. 'The way you just asked her out, that was sick!'

See also, *Ill*

Side boob (noun)

The visible left- or right-hand side of a woman's breast, usually the result of skimpy or loose-fitting clothing.

Side boob action (verb)

The opportunity of viewing side boobs. Usually occurs on holiday, on a televised red carpet premiere or when a bra-less girl wears a sleeveless T-shirt.

Sitch (noun)

Street way of saying situation.

E.g. 'What's the sitch, bitch?'

Skank (noun)

Derogatory term for a female who is at least two of the following:
- Promiscuous
- Sleazy
- Trashy
- Tacky
- Unhygienic
- Drug-dependant
- Alcoholic
- The subject of a sex tape

NB, a skank is like a slut, but more unsanitary.

See also, *Minger/minga, Ratchet, Skanky, Slag, Slapper, Slore, THOT*

Skanky (adjective)

Someone or something that is dirty, scruffy, unhygienic or promiscuous.

Usually, but not exclusively, followed by these words: 'bitch', 'ho'.

Sometimes followed by the word sofa or armchair when describing a piece of furniture that has unidentified stains on it.

Skeasy (adjective)

Someone who combines the character traits of being *sketchy* and sleazy.

Sketchy (adjective)

The replacement term for 'dodgy', sketchy is used to describe something or someone that makes you feel nervous or uncomfortable. It can also refer to something that's a grey area when it comes to what's legal or acceptable behaviour. A person who's sketchy is someone who gives you a bad feeling rather than someone who is actually a creep.

E.g. 'There was something about him that wasn't quite right. It might have been his missing sister or his blood-splattered clothes but I can't put my finger on it. All I know it that he was really sketchy.'

See also, *Shady*

Sket (noun)

A *Slapper* of absolute *skanky* proportions.

Skunk-eye (noun)

A glare of disgust, disdain or hatred.

See also, *Stank-eye*

Slacker (adjective)

Someone capable of working hard, but doesn't – and doesn't care.

Slag (adhective)

See *slapper*

Slammin' (adjective)

Something that's particularly impressive. Traditionally used to describe a piece of music, a party or a *hot* girl.

Slapper (noun)

A girl whose main ambition in life is to enter *Guinness World Records* under 'most one-night stands'. There is a high likelihood that someone desorbed as a slapper will also be described as being *fugly*.

See also, *Minger/minga, Ratchet, Slag, Skank, THOT*

Slay (verb)

Another word for dominating a competition.

See also, *Kill, Smash it*

Slore (adjective)

Cross between a slut and a whore; someone who will go to bed with anyone who has a shadow.

Smashed (adjective)

See *hammered*

Smash it (verb)

To be extremely successful at something, usually something of a competitive nature. Phrase beloved of idiotic *X-Factor* judges who can't think of anything original or meaningful to say.

See also, *Kill, Slay*

SMD (interjection)

Suck my dick. Used as an insult rather than a request for sexual favours.

See also, *GTH, GFY*

SMH (interjection)

Shaking (or shakes) my head – used to emphasise that a comment or action was unbelievably dumb or stupid.

E.g.

Friend: 'I can't hang tonight. I'm watching *Question Time*, bro.'

You: 'SMH.'

Snap it (verb)

To action of posting a photo or video clip on Snapchat.

E.g.

'That hilarious video you took of Karly swallowing her own sick. You should so snap it!'

SNOE (verb)

See *said no one ever.*

SOL (interjection)

Shit outta luck – the state you will find yourself in after getting 'Satan's Nazis' tattooed on your forehead and a giant penis tattooed on each cheek, then trying to find gainful employment.

Solid (adjective, noun, interjection)

(a) Something that's unbelievably cool or awesome.
E.g. 'That Eddie Murphy movie was solid! NB, no one will ever say this.
(b) A favour carried out for someone.
E.g. 'I need money for the night bus. Do me a solid.'
(c) Response to a statement to express agreement, satisfaction
    or approval.
E.g. You: 'I just got off with Mrs Mitchell in the chemistry lab!'
Friend: 'Solid!'

Sor-ree! (interjection)

What to say when you want to make a very patronising fauxpology.
See also, *Soz*

Soz (adjective, interjection)

Apologising or expressing regret with a complete lack of conviction.
See also, *Sor-ree!, Fauxpology*

Spaz attack (noun)

An intense episode of excitement and hyperactivity. While these can be triggered by feelings of intense joy they are more often aroused by feelings of anger, fear and resentment. Spaz attacks tend to occur when relationships go bad.

E.g. 'Tula found out Ty was cheating on her and had a mega-spaz attack.'

See also, *Spazzing out, Spazzy*

Spazzing out (noun)

The process of having a spaz attack.

See also, *Spazzy, Spaz attack*

Spazzy (adjective)

This can refer to someone who is over-energetic, but more commonly it describes someone who overreacts in an aggressive way to a given situation.

E.g. 'So I dropped your phone down the toilet. There's no need to go batshit spazzy!'

See also, *Batshit, Lose your shit, Spaz attack, Spazzing out*

Spit swap (verb)

The act of an open-mouthed kiss that involves massaging each other's tongues. Also known as a *Frenchie/frenchy, Suck face*

Spot-tease (noun)

A parking spot that appears to be free but as you approach it you realise it's actually been taken by a small car, or a car shittily parked that takes up its own space and about 20 per cent of the one next to it.

E.g. 'Shit! That Smart Car is a total spot-tease!'

Squad (noun)

A group of your closest friends. The term tends to be used by someone wanting to pretend they're *urban*.

See also, *Fam, Main/Mains, Peeps*

Squad goals (noun)

The collective aims and objectives of a group of friends; these should be aspirational rather than just intentions.

E.g. 'I was thinking more about us all getting places at uni rather than getting addicted to crystal meth or getting knocked up and moving into a council flat. That's not what I call squad goals!'

Stan (noun)

An insanely obsessed overzealous admirer or fan. A Stan (after the Eminem song of the same name) is the sort of person who has a picture of their idol tattooed over their back, who has crawled through ventilation ducts to get into their target's hotel room or who legally changes their name to something like 'Mrs Justin Bieber'.

See also, *Batshit crazy, Stanning*

Standard (adjective)

Some statements or comments are so comprehensible or obvious there's absolutely no point in commenting on them. However, if you absolutely, positively have to make some remark then 'standard' can be used in lieu of saying, 'Yes, that definitely goes without saying.'

E.g.

You: You up for the all-you-can-eat burrito buffet?'

Friend: 'Standard.'

Stank-eye (noun)

A more intense version of the *skunk-eye* or *stink-eye* in which you demonstrate a facial expression that looks like you really can smell shit.

Stanning (verb)

The act of being crazily obsessed with someone.
    See also, *Stan*

Starbies (noun)

Affectionate nickname for the nationwide coffee chain that pioneered two things; signature roasts and convincing people that a £2.50 cup of coffee represents good value.

Staycay (noun)

Short for staycation, e.g. staying at home or locally during a holiday period, nearly always through need (lack of money) rather than choice.

Steeze (adjective)

A great compliment to receive, inferring a combination of style and ease.
    E.g. 'Check out that grandmaster's chess moves. He got real steeze.'

STFU (interjection)

Shut the fuck up – often preceded by the word 'please' to indicate that it's said without a real sense of hostility. Used when someone is persistently sending online messages and you're busy.
    E.g.
    Friend: 'FFS you there, dude? Just sent u 17 texts about nudie pix Ellie just posted by mistake!!!'
    You: 'I'm in the library. Please STFU.'

Stink-eye (noun)

See *skunk-eye*, *stank-eye*

Stoked (adjective)

To be *über* enthusiastic about something; a state of excitement and anticipation almost to the point of rapture.
　See also, *Amp'd/amp'd up, Amped, Pumped, Psyched*

Street (noun)

Anything that alludes to an over-romanticised urban culture/ lifestyle that includes hip-hop, gangstas, skateboarding, BMX, hustling, graffiti, tattoos, parkour and *hangin'*.
　See also, *Ghetto, Urban*

Stressmas (noun)

An annual festival culminating on 25 December that celebrates the birth of Jesus, crass commercialism, binge-drinking, gluttony and shit programmes on TV.

Stride of pride (noun)

Like the *walk of shame* but carried out with less shame and more gusto.

Struggle bus (noun)

Metaphor to describe a situation you're finding very difficult.
　E.g. 'I've got to write two thousand words on the social and economic consequences of the dissolution of the monasteries for Tuesday and I'm really riding the struggle bus.'

Strugglas (noun)

Someone who struggles with something (rhymes with 'Douglas').

Strugs (noun)

The effect of struggling with something.
E.g. 'Damn! All that history stuff is giving me *über* strugs.'

Stunting (verb)

The act of posing or shamelessly flaunting your wealth in the form of designer clothes, bling or an exotic car.

Stupid o'clock (noun)

An unreasonable time of day to be asked to do or attend something i.e. any time before 10 a.m.

Suck/sucks (verb)

To be inadequate or astonishingly terrible.
    See also, *Blows, Blows Chunks*

Sucka (noun)

A catch-all term for someone gullible who's been tricked or scammed in some way; can also refer to someone who's been hurt physically or verbally.
    See also, *Own, Owned*

Suckage (noun)

An abstract measurement of how much someone or something sucks.
    E.g. 'Did you see *The Voice* last night. Man. That was maximum suckage!'

Suck face (verb)

Hardcore snogging, traditionally involving the swapping of saliva.
    See also *Frenchie, Get off, Make out, Spit Swap*

Suckfest (noun)

Something that absolutely and positively, without any shade of a doubt, *sucks*.

E.g.

'A whole day traipsing round that gallery looking at Pre-Raphaelite art. Man, what a *gimongous* suckfest!'

Sucktacular (adjective)

Something that *sucks* on such a dramatic and impressive level that the degree of *suckage* will be almost impossible to surpass.

Suck up (noun, verb)

To be over-complimentary and sycophantic in order to get something, e.g. a favour, friendship or promotion.

E.g.

Wannabe friend: 'Hey, girl. I just love those leopard-print biker boots. And that chain belt. It's so savage.'

You [under breath]: 'Suck up.'

See also, *Begfriend/beg friend*

Sup? (Interjection)

See *Zup?*

Swag (adjective, noun)

A word with a multitude of meanings, all of which are overused by *douches*:

(a) The state of being stylish or cool, e.g. 'Zayn Malik? Really? I got more swag in my ass than that guy.'

(b) A term for fashionable clothes and accessories, e.g. 'Did you see Evie at the gig? She was wearing some killa swag.'

(c) A way of describing self-assurance or confidence, e.g. 'After she dumped Stevo she totally got her swag back.'

See also *Amazeballs, Cool, Dope, Killer, Savage*

Swag points (noun)

An abstract way of comparing and contrasting just how dope anyone is. In other words, the currency of cool. When someone does something swag-worthy they are nominally rewarded with swag points. Likewise, if they do something uncool they lose swag points.

E.g. 'I caught that dude listening to Coldplay. That is such a major loss of swag points.'

Sweet (adjective, interjection)

Said in response to a statement or after observing an action, this is an indication of total agreement or admiration.

See also, *Solid*

Swole (adjective)

Someone's who's very muscular and in good physical shape, usually as a result of excessive working out at the gym or in prison.

See also, *Built, Buff, Fit, Hench, Reem, Ripped*

Sympathy boner (noun)

An unplanned and embarrassing erection that occurs when a male is hugging a female friend to console her about some trauma in her life (which, ninety-nine out of a hundred times, will involve her or one of her *mains* being dumped by or cheated on by someone known to the owner of the sympathy boner).

See also, *Boner*

Tag hag (noun)

Someone obsessed with buying and wearing designer clothing. Usually believes they are a better person for doing so.

See also, *Label whore*

Talk to the hand! (interjection)

A way of totally ignoring and disregarding someone's criticism. The phrase is usually accompanied by raising your hand and holding it, palm facing outwards, towards whoever you're addressing. To be used when you can't think of a witty comeback or reasoned argument.

Talkward (adjective)

Feeling of agonising awkwardness that descends over two people who meet up after a long period of time and soon realise that they have virtually nothing to say to one another.

Friend: 'Hey, Kobie!'

You: 'Joel!'

Friend: 'How's things? You still at . . . er . . . ?'

You: 'Not any more . . . What about you? Still with . . . er . . . ?'

Friend: 'Nah . . .'

You: 'Oh . . .'

Friend: 'Yeah...'

You: 'You still see Renza and Taylor?'

Tag hag

Friend: 'No. You?'

You: 'Not for years . . .'

Friend: 'So . . . '

You: 'Hey. That's my bus . . . gotta dash.'

Friend: 'F' sho. Let's do this again.'

You: 'Solid!' [to yourself]: 'Man, that was talkward.'

See also, *Nonversation*

Tanarexia (noun)

Disorder in which a person has an obsessive need for fake tans. Tends to be the type of person who uses *reem* in their conversations.

Tard (noun)

Someone so retarded in their behaviour that they don't even deserve the addition of the prefix 're'. NB, in this sense, retarded refers to acting like a *douche* rather than implying any mental impairment.

See also, *Dumbtard, Fucktard*

Tat (noun)

Tattoo.

See also, *Ink*

Tatted (verb)

To have been tattooed.

Tekkers (noun)

To have tekkers is to have particular skills or a technique. This can apply to computer programming, skateboarding, gaming, football, dancing, mixed martial arts, Sudoku, flower arranging, Candy

Crush – anything. Someone who demonstrates a complete lack of ability in a particular area is said to have 'no tekkers'.

Televoidance (noun)

The act of avoiding speaking to someone by pretending to be on your phone as they approach you.

Warning: There is a danger of being *busted* if, when you're on the fake call, your phone starts ringing for real.

TFFO (interjection)

Totally fucking full out/on – to do something with an unbelievable level of commitment; to go above and beyond all expectations.

See also, *Go hard or go home*

That's long (interjection)

Used to describe something that requires the expenditure of an unacceptable amount of effort or time.

E.g.

Friend: 'Hey. Come over later. We can do my four-thousand-piece jigsaw of Rita Ora.'

You: 'Ugh! That's loooong.'

Thesbian (noun)

Someone who isn't actually a lesbian, but who acts like one.

Thirsty (adjective)

Not a desire or craving for liquid nourishment, power or knowledge, but a reference to someone's over-eagerness or more likely, desperation.

E.g.

'Ugh! That zit guy has been following me around all evening. He is so thirsty.'

THOT (noun)

That ho over there – term of abuse that implies that a girl is sexually promiscuous.

See also, *Skank*

Throw shade (verb)

Ruthlessly insulting or judging someone; showing an unbelievable amount of sass.

E.g.

Friend: 'Yo momma's so fat, when she jumped in the air she got stuck.'

You: 'Bruv, why you throwing shade at my momma?'

Thumpage (noun)

A measurement of unrelenting heavy bass. NB, that's bass as in low-frequency sound, not bass as in the fish belonging to the perch family.

Tick (adjective)

Someone so attractive that it's almost a crime.

See also, *Buff, Hot, Hott, Fit, Peng, Reem, Swole*

Tidy (adjective)

Something that is better than being merely good. Sometimes used in place of *cool*.

Tight (adjective)

(a) Something that's cool, awesome, stylish or fashionable, e.g. 'Hey, Stephanié. Those spotty tights are tight!'

(b) A close friendship, e.g. 'Me and Raheem; we tight.'

TILF (noun)

Teacher I'd like to fuck – any teacher/lecturer you find physically attractive and sexually desirable. NB, if you're under sixteen this is best kept as a fantasy rather than something to be acted on.

TLDR/TL;DR (interjection)

Too long, didn't read – describes something that you're just too lazy to look at. Usually refers to anything longer than 140 characters.

TMI (interjection)

Too much information – a level of knowledge about someone that leaves you feeling disturbed, uncomfortable or disgusted. Usually involves your parents and sex.
　　See also, *Overshare*

TOF (noun)

Ton of fun – a plus-plus sized girl. Used as a term of affection rather than an insult.

Tool (noun)

This usually refers to a male who meets one or more of these criteria:
- Is incompetent, stupid or useless.
- Tries far too hard to impress.
- Has an over-inflated ego and thinks of himself as a *player*.
- Is easily influenced or manipulated by others.
E.g.
You: 'So you dated her for a month, took her to the best restaurants and even bought her a whole stack of new outfits and shit. Then she goes and dumps your sorry ass!'
　　Friend: 'I was such a tool.'
　　See also, *Loser, Douche, Douchbag*

Tool bag (noun)

Someone who is such a *tool* that the word tool alone doesn't do justice to his idiocy or sense of over-inflated self-worth. The phrase 'tool bag' can imply either that the person is a whole collection of tools or that he's a cross between a *tool* and a *douchebag*.

Top bantz (noun)

Particularly insightful or mocking banter. Less commonly described as '*epic* bantz'.
  See also, *Bantz*

Totes, totz (adverb, interjection)

A way for teenage girls to say the word 'totally' with the twin advantages of appearing cool and also saving time. Can also be used to signify that you agree with a statement.
  E.g.
  Bianca: 'That guy with the ginger dreads who works in Starbies is totes cute.'
  Shaznee: 'Totes.'

Totes adorbs (adjective, interjection)

Way of describing something that causes delight, excitement or general giddiness due to the fact that it is totally adorable. This phrase can be used in context with many things, from kittens to pert buttocks.

Totz/totes me goats/m'goats (adverb, interjection)

Another way to say, 'I absolutely agree with everything you've just said.'
  See also, *Aight, Church*

Train wreck (noun)

Someone whose life is in complete and utter disarray; think of their whole existence as just one monumental *epic fail*. Unlike a *hot mess* there is absolutely nothing appealing or even remotely intriguing about this sort of person. Nothing at all.

Can also be used to describe an event or action that is an unmitigated disaster.

E.g. 'Marlon can't get a job or get laid. He's got zits, a lisp, a limp, bad breath and that third nipple thing going on. Oh, yeah. And he's ginger. His life is just one total train wreck.'

Tramp stamp (noun)

Derogatory term for a tattoo on a girl's lower back/hip area which usually takes the form of a butterfly, tribal symbols or Chinese characters that are meant to spell out, 'happiness', 'respect' or 'joy' but which actually mean 'king prawns in lemon sauce'. And remember, just because you have a bible quote inscribed above your arse doesn't make you look any less of a *skank*.

Trending (verb)

Anything that's currently popular and which you must discuss in order to appear cool.

See also, *Bang on trend, on trend*

Trippy (adjective)

Something that's either very weird or very cool. Or both.

Troll (noun)

Someone who acts in a confrontational or hateful manner on social media in order to annoy, outrage, provoke and upset. Also known as a *douchebag*.

Trolling (verb)

The act of being a *fucktard* online.

Trump (noun)

A really shitty haircut that looks like you did it yourself with blunt scissors and didn't use a mirror.

TTYL (interjection)

Talk to you later – sign off to a message which saves you typing, 'Now you're boring me.'

Turnt (adjective)

    (a) Someone who is hammered, wasted or fucked up.
    (b) An event that's fantastic fun.
    E.g. 'Bro, that party was so turnt! An hour in and I was turnt!'
    See also, *Crunk, Hammered, Sauced, Shitfaced*

Twat (noun)

Can be used as an acronym for 'the war against terror' but more usually used as an alternative word for the vagina or as an insult.
    See also, *Douche, Douchebag, Twot*

Twatted (adjective)

    (a) To be extremely drunk (another word for *crunk, faded, hammered, lit, trashed, turnt, wasted*).
    (b) To be severely beaten, usually involving some sort of blow to the head.

Tweeps (noun)

Confusingly this can mean both anyone with a twitter account or the followers of someone's twitter account (usually a celebrity).

Twercules (noun)

Someone (male or female) who is supremely skilled in the art of twerking; so-called because of their flawless, almost god-like ability to wiggle their buttocks.

See also, *Twerk, Twerking*

Twerk, Twerking (noun, verb)

Provocative rhythmic dancing that features the gyration of the hips and shaking of the buttocks up-and-down and left-to-right. The move previously known as 'shakin' yo' ass'.

See also, *Twercules*

Twisted (noun)

This can mean all of the following:
- (a) Drunk.
- (b) Under the influence of drugs.
- (c) Completely messed up (physically, mentally, ethically or morally).
- (d) Insanely crazy or wild.

Meanings (a) and (b) usually lead to (c) and (d).

TWSS (interjection)

That's what she said – a phrase that immature boys and men just have to make whenever someone says something that could be perceived as sexual innuendo.

E.g.
You: 'How was the French exam?'
Friend: 'It was long and hard and I struggled with the oral.'
You: 'TWSS.'

TWOT (noun)

An alternative spelling of *twat* but also an acronym for 'total waste of time'.

E.g.
Friend: 'Antony on drums? TWOT!'
You: 'Agree. What a twot.'

Typeractive (adjective)

Anyone who spends an abnormal (and possibly obsessive) amount of time texting, emailing, facebooking, messaging or tweeting.

Urban (adjective)

Fashionable term used to describe black culture, music or fashion without actually using the word 'black'. There is an inverse relationship between how white/suburban someone is and how desperate they are to fit in with the urban lifestyle.

See also, *Gangsta, Ghetto, Street*

Über (adjective)

Not the name given to the ubiquitous minicab service so beloved of teenagers but a prefix that means 'very', in order to add emphasis. In this context it implies something is the absolute ultimate e.g. über-*noob*, über-*sick*, über-*hot*, über-*bantz*, über-*epic*, über-*hammered* etc., etc., etc., etc.

Over use of the term is considered über-*lame.*

Überlicious (adjective)

Something that's extremely tasty and satisfying . . . but not quite as tasty or appetizing as *deligious*.

Übershopper (adjective)

A compulsive shopper. Someone who finds it almost impossible to stop *poppin' tags.*

Uey (noun)

Pronounced 'yoo-ey', this when you're walking down the street, realise you're going the wrong way and make a sudden 180-degree change of direction.

Ugly radius/ugly range (noun)

The distance from you that someone stops looking attractive. This will vary according to personal tastes and preferences and the impact of clothes and/or make-up. One of the effects of alcohol is its ability to significantly reduce the ugly radius.

E.g.

Girl: 'Jono's only good-looking from across the class. Ten feet is about his ugly radius. Closer than that his face is zit city.'

See also, *HFFA*

Uggs/uggz (adjective)

Ugly. Not to be confused with the Australian footwear brand UGG, although many feel the words are interchangeable.

Ugly sleep (noun)

When you wake from a deep, deep sleep with dried drool and/or sheet or pillow creases ingrained on your face.

Ugmo (adjective, noun)

This can mean something or someone very ugly (but not as ugly as *fugly)* or can be used as a general term of abuse without necessarily referencing someone's appearance. Derives from the words 'ugly motherfucker' although some with a more childish disposition claim it's derived from the phrase 'ugly monster'.

E.g. 'Hey – you in the bushes! Stop flashing me, ugmo!'

Ugmania (noun)

The legendary homeland of all *ugmos*.

Unfriend (verb)

As *de-friend* however this term can also mean ending a real-life rather than a virtual friendship.

Ungood (adjective)

Bad but in a very understated way, to draw attention to just how bad something really is.
E.g.
Villain: 'So, Mr Bond. In less than sixty seconds a 5000-volt charge will electrify your testicles, a vat of concentrated hydrochloric acid will be tipped over your head and your ears will be assaulted by the first Celine Dion album.'
James Bond: 'Hmmm – that is totz ungood.'

Unpossible (adjective)

Something that's even more impossible than impossible.

Upchuck (verb)

See *barf, ralph*

Up for it (verb)

To be ready or prepared for something. That something usually means sex.

V-card (noun, verb)

Virginity as a physical object.

    E.g.

    You: 'So my parents were out last night, Sherry came back to mine and I stamped her V-card!'

    Friend: 'Hey! That's my sister!'

    You: 'Meh.'

Vacay (noun)

Holiday; vacation.

Vaguebooking (verb)

Posting an ambiguous status on Facebook that prompts friends to ask what's happening. Can be used to attract attention or can be an authentic cry for help.

    E.g.

    Friend: 'Dude! Did you see Mikey's status: "Kidnappers breaking down my door!!! This is last thing I can type before they get in and . . . "'

You: 'Yeah, That Mikey! Always vaguebooking.'

Versace (adjective)

Something that's cool, desirable, very, very expensive and exclusive, e.g. 'Did you see that black Maserati? So Versace!'

NB, there is no point in using this word to describe anything made by Versace.

VFC (adjective)

Very fucking cold – use this acronym when your fingers are too cold to actually type the words in full.

Vibe (noun)

A feeling about something or someone or the general atmosphere in a place.

NB, vibe is not used to describe the actual physical atmosphere. That would sound wrong and very unscientific if used in say, a geography exam, e.g. 'The Earth's vibe is 78 per cent nitrogen.'

Vibe killer (noun)

Someone who turns up uninvited or unexpected to a social event and completely destroys the fantastic time you were having. Usually an ex or your parents.

Vidiot (noun)

Someone who plays videogames excessively and assumes the expression of a simpleton; someone with a glazed expression and total unawareness of his surroundings.

See also, *Mouse potato*

Vurp (noun, verb)

A burp that, to your surprise, is immediately followed by a small amount of vomit appearing in your mouth.

Wack (adjective)

Something that's pathetic, uncool, fake, crazy, irrational or of questionable quality. Also, something that *blows chunks*.

See also, *Lame*

Waddup? (interjection)

See *Wassup?*

Walk of shame (noun)

Entering your house, dorm, place of work etc., with your hair dishevelled, wearing the same clothes as the previous day; an indication you had an unplanned one-night stand or a booty call.

See also, *Stride of Pride*

Wallin' (verb)

To sit or stand against a wall at a party.

E.g.

Friend: 'Don't you want to play musical chairs or grandma's foosteps?'

You: 'No, man. I just chillin' and wallin'.'

Wanker (noun)

See *Douche, Douchebag*

Wanksta (adjective, noun)

A *wannabe* gangsta who pretends to live the *BAMF* lifestyle but who is completely *fake*. A wanksta is usually middle-class, lives in the suburbs, listens to Eminem and Jay Z, has learned life skills from playing *Grand Theft Auto* and pretends to be *ghetto* by ending his sentences with the phrase 'an' shit'. Sometimes spelt 'wangsta'.

See also, *Gangsta, Loser*

Wannabe (noun)

Someone who tries too hard to fit in with another group of people – copying their fashion, their actions and even the way they talk.

E.g. 'Look at him with his saggy pants, boxers showing and belt hangin' round his sorry ass. He's not even qualified to be a douche. He's a douche wannabe!'

See also, *Tool*

Wasbian (noun)

See *Hasbian, Yestergay*

Wassup? (interjection)

A quick way to ask 'What's going on?' or 'What has been going on?' Can also be used as a general greeting instead in place of 'Hello' or 'Hi'. Can also be abbreviated to *Sup?* or *Zup?*

See also, *What up? Waddup? Wazzup?*

Wasted (adjective)

Heavily intoxicated or under the influence of drugs. Or both simultaneously.

See also, *Crunk, Faded, Trashed, Turnt, Wasted*

Wanksta

Wasteman (noun)

Someone who does nothing with his or her life and by inference is a total waste of space. Often applied to videogame playing *slackers* who usually go on to found tech companies and earn billions and billions of *scrilla*.

Wax (noun)

A vinyl record (seven-inch or LP).

Wazzup? (interjection)

See *what up?, Sup?, Waddup? Wassup? Zup?*

Wedgie/wedgy (noun)

The act of grabbing the waistband of someone's underwear from behind and suddenly pulling it up as high as possible. This is funnier than it sounds.

Welc/welcs/welcy (interjection)

A quick way to say 'You're welcome.'
 E.g.
 Friend: 'Thanks for that great book, *How to Talk Teen*.'
 You: 'Welcs.'

Well (adjective)

The 'in' way of saying 'extremely', 'very' or 'really'.
 Most commonly used to prefix the words 'jel', 'pleased' and 'hard'. Hardly ever used in front of the word 'read' since few teenagers know people who have gained extensive knowledge from reading widely.
 See also, *Totes/totz*

Whatever! (interjection)

(a) The correct way to end an argument or confrontation when you realise that you're wrong but don't want to admit it. Think of it as a polite way of saying, 'Fuck you'. 'Whatever!' automatically brings the discussion to an end; however, to add emphasis to your statement either present your flat palm to those you were talking to or toss your hair.

(b) A statement that signifies your complete indifference/apathy.

(c) A reply to parents which means, 'Please tell me I'm adopted.'

See also, *Meh, Whatev/whatevs, Whevs*

Whatev/whatevs (interjection)

A way of saying '*Whatever!*' that implies greater flippancy or scorn.

What up? (interjection)

See also, *Sup?, Wassup?, Wazzup?, Wuddup?, Zup?*

Whevs (interjection)

A way of saying *whatevs* that indicates your complete and utter contempt for what's been discussed and the fact that you're only willing to waste one syllable on a response.

Whipped (adjective)

See *pussy-whipped*

Whole nother thing (noun)

Cool way of saying, 'And now, on a completely different subject . . .'

Wicked (adjective)

Cool or awesome. Usually preceded by the word 'well' to add emphasis.

See also, *Amazeballs, Awesome, Brill, Chill, Dope, Fly, Hip, Kickass, Killer*

Wi-five (noun, verb)

A *high five* greeting made while texting or involved in any form of online conversation.

See also *Air five*

Wikiwhore (noun)

Someone addicted to checking details on Wikipedia, often using it just to be able to insert obscure facts into conversation to appear interesting.

E.g.

You: 'Coming to the mall?'

Friend: 'Sho'. Did you know that Britain's first shopping mall was Birmingham's Bull Ring, opening on 29 May 1964? At the time it was the largest indoor shopping centre in Europe, with a total floor area of 23 acres. Inspired by American suburban malls, the Bull Ring promised "coatless shopping" in an air-conditioned environment that was maintained at "late spring" temperatures.'

You: 'Wikiwhore!'

Friend: 'Launched on 15 January 2001, Wikipedia initially offered . . .'

Wimp (noun)

See *pussy*

Wimp out (verb)

To back out of a situation in a cowardly way.
> E.g.
> You: 'So, laters we're gonna go for ten pints and a vindaloo.'
> Friend: 'Er . . . tonight's my pottery class . . .'
> You: 'Don't wimp out on me, man!'

Wood (noun)

Another word for *boner*.

Woodache (noun)

Pain and soreness from too much sexual exertion (either by yourself or with a partner).

WOL (noun)

Waste of life. An insult that is usually followed by the phrase, 'I hope you DIAF.'

Word/word up (noun)

An out-dated term to signify that you agree with or approve of what someone has just said. If you go to church it's the equivalent of saying, 'Amen.' 'Word' has now largely been replaced by *cool beans*.

Wordrobe (noun)

Another name for your vocabulary.
> E.g. 'Hey, mister. You swallow a dictionary? You got an extensive wordrobe.'

Wordrobe malfunction (noun)

Accidentally swearing during a conversation with a person or group that might be easily offended.

E.g.

You: 'So I lifted the bonnet and there was smoke everywhere. That's when I realised the engine was fucked . . . sorry, I mean ruined.'

Vicar: 'That's all right son. You just had a wordrobe malfunction.'

Wotev, wotevs (interjection)

See *whatev, whatevs*

WTF! (interjection)

What the fuck – universal phrase to express any of the following:

- Anger
- Disbelief
- Amazement
- Irritation
- Confusion
- Wonder
- Suspicion
- Surprise

Although WTF! Is usually used as a response at the end of a sentence it can also be used to begin a question, e.g. 'WTF you lookin' at?'

Wuddup? (Interjection)

A variation of *wassup?*

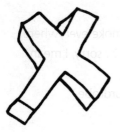

Xmaxed (adjective)

The unwelcome state where your credit card is maxed out after buying Christmas presents for everyone.

Yard (noun)

Not just your back garden but a term for your whole home or neighbourhood.
  See also, *Endz*

Yas!/yasss! (interjection)

Expression of affirmation or delight that means so much, much, much, much, much, much more than a mere 'Yes!' (and far quicker to type than 'Yessssssssss!!!'

Yello (interjection)

Combination of 'Yes?' and 'Hello'; a hip way of answering the phone.

Yestergay (noun)

Term used to denote someone who used to be, but is no longer, homosexual.
  See also, *Hasbian, Wasbian*

Yo (pronoun)

Your. Usually precedes the word 'momma' to introduce an insult that alludes to her excessive weight.

Yo! (interjection)

Universal form of greeting in place of 'Hi', 'Hey', 'Hello' or 'How do you do?' Usually used excessively by deluded white middle-class kids in nice suburbs who think they're *street*.

YOLO (interjection)

You only live once – advice to the effect that you should enjoy the present moment without worrying about the consequences. Usually used as a rationale for reckless and impulsive behaviour that will result in injury or death. However, YOLO is often used incorrectly when describing mundane activities with no real degree of risk.

Incorrect usage
- 'I just ate five Big Macs and a Filet-O-Fish! YOLO!'
- 'I just took an hour's nap! YOLO!'
- 'I just wrote the names of Little Mix on my arm in biro. YOLO!'

Correct usage
- 'After eight pints let's try and leap between these two seventh-floor balconies. Why? Because YOLO!'
- 'Why would I want to eat a live tarantula? YOLO, that's why.'
- 'I'm going to raise Satan and then form a death cult that sacrifices babies but YOLO, right?'

NB, YOLO never, ever, ever stands for 'you obviously love omelettes'.

Yoloing (verb)

The act of participating in a particularly hazardous, exciting or stupid activity, e.g. 'I'm going to be yoloing to the max later when I go cliff-diving with a whole pile of scorpions shoved down my pants.'

Youngify (verb)

To make someone look younger by the use of Photoshop or to lie about your own age, usually for personal gain.

E.g. 'It wasn't 'til I met his twin sister that I realise he'd youngified himself on his profile. Turns out he's thirty-eight, not seventeen. What a perv!'

YouTube degree (noun)

Self-certified qualification awarded when you've watched enough YouTube instructional videos on a given topic that you feel you're an expert.

E.g.

Friend: 'And you're certain you can carry out the procedure?'

You: 'Fo' sho. I've got a YouTube Degree in doing appendectomies.'

YouTube hole (noun)

What you fall into when you become obsessed by vlogs or instructional videos.

E.g. 'I was looking at DIY eyebrow-threading. Next thing I know, I've watched thirty-two videos and it's 3 a.m! Shit! I'd fallen into a deep YouTube hole.'

YOYO (interjection)

You're on your own – possible response to a YOLO suggestion.

E.g.

Friend: 'Let's break into the zoo and punch a tiger. YOLO!'

You: 'YOYO!'

Za (noun)

Abbreviation for pizza that no self-respecting person actually uses. Well, there are some that do, but they're also the same people who also say *Zert*. Hit them in the head with a shovel.

Zert/zert (noun)

Dessert.

Zing! (interjection)

What to say to someone to highlight the fact that you've just made an extremely sarcastic or witty comment or comeback. Often used in a *dis* or *top bantz*. When used in a group scenario the zing is often celebrated by a *high five*.
E.g.
Friend: 'What did you do last night?'
You: 'Your sister. Zing!'

Zombie Jesus Day (noun)

A cooler name for Easter.

Zombie leg (noun)

When one or both legs have gone to sleep so that, instead of walking, you stagger around like a reanimated corpse. This condition usually occurs after you've been sitting in a contorted position or if you've been on the toilet for too long.

Zombie lie (noun)

A lie that absolutely refuses to die no matter how many times it's disproven; or – years after it was laid to rest – rises up again.

E.g.

Friend: 'Everyone keeps telling me that you cried your eyes out at the end of *Marley & Me*.'
You: 'Fucking zombie lie!'

Zup? (interjection)

Used when you don't have time to ask, '*Wassup?*' Can be used as a question or as a general greeting and is usually (but not exclusively) followed by the words 'man', 'bro', 'bruv', 'bruvva' or 'dude'.

See also, *Sup?*

Eurrgh!

Mark Leigh

Available to buy in ebook and paperback

When in Rome, don't do as the Romans do... don't go in the first place! An hilarious guide to Europe's most dreadful destinations!

Ignoring the fact that the EU is a grotesque, officious money sucking totalitarian machine that devours national sovereignty and pukes out unwanted, unwelcome and intrusive legislation, there's a whole variety of other reasons including: national costumes that are as preposterous as they are pointless; Polish spelling; drivers who view speed limits as targets rather than warnings; yodelling; bouzouki music; donkey abuse; using a comma as a decimal point; Eurodisco; Eurovision; and in fact anything else preceded by the word 'Euro' (apart from Euro sceptic).

This is less of a guidebook and more of a warning.

Colour Me Bad

ILYA

Available to buy in ebook and paperback

Strees out, colour in, deface, obliterate and take out your
frustrations on the page!

Putting the stress back into colouring books, this is your
chance to colour outside of the lines, to rip, rend, tear
and destroy, scribble, deface or destroy the images. Evil
Editor ILYA I. KILLYA has assembled a crack team of top
professional cartoonists and illustrators to 'toon up your
terrors, throw out your troubles and definitively trash
your traumas.

Fill in these visual fillips, images of stress – distressed bods,
stressful situations, the daily tripe that messes with your
melons – and end it, any way you care to, however you dare
to: get creative, be artistic, play anarchic. Feel free to go as
twisted or rude as you like!

The Mammoth Book of Tasteless and Outrageous Lists

Karl Shaw

Available to buy in ebook and paperback

A truly mammoth collection of weird and gross trivia about sex, death and everything in between.

Prepare to be even more revolted, flabbergasted, appalled and entertained by this incredible follow-up collection of bizarre but absolutely true trivia. Nothing is too distasteful for this astonishing compendium, including scores of eclectic lists to amuse, astonish and appal your friends. Entries include:

10 Road-kill Recipes

History's 10 Most Murderous Regimes

10 Historic Sex Toys

10 People who Married Their Nieces

10 Deaths by Sex

10 People Killed by Falling Animals

The Mammoth Book of Weird Records

Jim Theobald

Available to buy in ebook and paperback

Too wacky for conventional record books – do not try this at home!

Everyone's heard of Usain Bolt, but how many people know about Dineka Maguire? Like Bolt, the Irishwoman is a world record holder but in the rather lesser known sport of bog snorkelling. She is just one of the hundreds of unsung heroes featured in this book chronicling those who go to bizarre lengths to break world records in the weirdest categories; people who devote hours of intense training to spitting dung, eating cockroaches, sniffing feet or tossing tuna in the hope of one day being recognised as the best in the world. This astonishing compendium of the oddest, wackiest and most disgusting world records will amuse and astound in equal measure.

The Mammoth Book of Losers

Karl Shaw

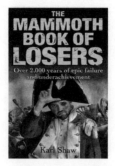

Available to buy in ebook and paperback

Over 2,000 years of epic failure and underachievement

This compendious celebration of ineptitude includes some of history's most spectacularly ill-conceived expeditions and entirely useless pursuits, and features tales of black comedy, insane foolhardiness, breathtaking stupidity and relentless perseverance in the face of inevitable defeat.

Entries include: briefest career in dentistry; least successful bonding exercise; most futile attempt to find a lost tribe; most pointless lines of research by someone who should have known better; least successful celebrity endorsement; least convincing excuse for a war; worst poetic tribute to a root vegetable; least successful display of impartiality by a juror; and least successful expedition by camel.

The Mammoth Book of More Dirty, Sick, X-Rated and Politically Incorrect Jokes

Geoff Tibballs

Available to buy in ebook and paperback

Funny, fearless and absolutely filthy – nearly 3,000 more uncensored, dirty, sick, and deeply politically incorrect jokes, covering just about every topic imaginable, from adultery to (sex in) zoos, including an assortment of bad taste lists. A worthy, all-new follow-on to the first bestselling volume.

The Good, The Bad and The Wurst

Geoff Tibballs

Available to buy in ebook and paperback

60 extraordinary years of Eurovision, from Celine Dion to Dustin the Turkey via Abba and Conchita Wurst – the drag acts, the bad acts and all the nul points heroes.

The Eurovision Song Contest has for ever existed in a parallel universe where a song about the construction of a hydro-electric power station is considered cutting-edge pop, where half a dozen warbling Russian grandmothers are considered Saturday night entertainment, where a tune repeating the word 'la' 138 times is considered a winner, and where Australia is considered part of Europe.

This book chronicles the 100 craziest moments in the history of Eurovision to capture some of the magic from this yearly event that continues to beguile and bemuse in equal measure – from 1957's scandal of a 13-second kiss to the 1976 Greek entry's savage indictment of Turkish foreign policy in Cyprus, plus all the sparkly costumes, terrible lyrics and tactical voting.

Crap Kitchen

Geoff Tibballs

Available to buy in ebook and paperback

The worst cookbook ever, packed with truly bizarre and utterly disgusting recipes from all over the world.

Ever since humankind produced its first foodie, the culinary world has dished up some staggering confections which could best be described as 'acquired tastes': dishes such as virgin boy eggs (eggs soaked in the urine of prepubescent boys); calf-brain custard; and beard beer, made from the yeast found in facial hair.

From the Roman Empire (grilled cow's womb) to modern-day China (tuna eyeball) via Sardinia (maggot-infested cheese) and Vietnam (the still-beating heart of a snake), this is the most revolting cookbook you'll ever read. Bon appétit!